THE PERGAMON ENGLISH LIBRARY

EDITORIAL DIRECTORS: GEORGE ALLEN AND BORIS FORD

EXECUTIVE EDITOR: ESMOR JONES

PUBLISHER: ROBERT MAXWELL, M.C., M.P.

THE RELUCTANT READER

THE
RELUCTANT READER

by

AIDAN CHAMBERS

1966
THE QUEEN'S AWARD
TO INDUSTRY 1966

PERGAMON PRESS

PERGAMON PRESS LTD.

OXFORD · LONDON · EDINBURGH
NEW YORK · TORONTO · SYDNEY

Copyright © 1969 Aidan Chambers
First edition 1969
Library of Congress Catalog Card No. 68–54930

Printed in Great Britain by A. Wheaton & Co., Exeter

08 013067 4

FOR S. H. LOOSLEY AND DAPHNE

Contents

Acknowledgements

USE of the following copyright material is acknowledged with thanks.

ERNEST ROE: *Teachers, Librarians and Children*; Crosby Lockwood & Son Ltd. (F. W. Cheshire Pty. Ltd., Melbourne).

Rave magazine; George Newnes Ltd.

Petticoat/Trend magazine; Fleetway Publications Ltd.

W. E. JOHNS: *Biggles and the Gun Runners*; Brockhampton Press Ltd.

BEVERLY CLEARY: *Fifteen*; Penguin Books Ltd.

JOHN WYNDHAM: *The Day of the Triffids*; Michael Joseph Ltd.

ARMSTRONG SPERRY: *The Boy Who Was Afraid*; Bodley Head Ltd.

BETTINA HÜRLIMANN (translator and editor, Brian Alderson): *Three Centuries of Children's Books in Europe*; Oxford University Press Ltd.

THE LIBRARY ASSOCIATION: *Chosen for Children*, edited by Marcus Crouch.

PHILIP TURNER: *The Grange at High Force*; Oxford University Press Ltd.

ALAN GARNER: *Elidor*; Wm. Collins & Sons Ltd.

CHILDREN'S BOOK CENTRE LTD.: *Children's Book News*, edited by Nancy Lockwood.

JOHN ROWE TOWNSEND: *Written for Children*; Garnet Miller Ltd.

ALAN SILLITOE: *Saturday Night and Sunday Morning*; W. H. Allen & Co.

ROBERT J. HOARE: *The Bookseller;* J. Whitaker & Son.

THE SCHOOL LIBRARY ASSOCIATION: *The School Librarian*, edited by Norman Furlong.

Most of all, I would like to thank all those who have contributed to this book by answering my questions, and by allowing me to quote their answers. Some are named, some remain in preferred anonymity. Naturally, the conclusions I draw from their comments and experience remain my responsibility, and do not necessarily imply acceptance of the same views on their part.

I would like to remember my debt to the young people and staff of Archway School, Stroud, Glos., where much of the experience which formed this book was gained; and to the Headmaster above all, to whom and to whose wife this book is affectionately dedicated.

AIDAN CHAMBERS

PART ONE

The Reader in the Red

I

The Submerged Sixty per cent

'FOR Heaven's sake, Philip,' I said, and I could hear the despair and exaspera-
tion in my voice, 'there must be *something* you will read!'

For a month, lesson after infuriated lesson, I had tried to find a book at
which Philip would not turn up his nose, finger through in desultory fashion
and return to me or the shelf with a weak smile. His excuses for 'that one'
varied. It didn't look exciting enough; it was too long, too big, or too young;
it was too hard to understand; he hadn't time just then; he didn't feel like
reading *that* sort of story today.

It was Philip's last term at school: he was 15 and 2 months, had a month
and a half left to his last day as a school boy, had a job fixed with a building
firm about which he had little apparent enthusiasm; and he came from a
home consisting of a much older motor-mechanic brother, a sister at the
local grammar school, and parents who found him 'difficult'. His performance at school was always worse than the intelligence displayed in his frequent
upsets and scrapes suggested it ought to be. In a four-stream, traditional
secondary modern, he sat firmly and comfortably in the lower half of the
'C' form. He was, in everything academic or 'schoolly', reluctant. The
library and reading for Philip were no exceptions.

And so, at the end of a desperate 'push' to make Philip at least a willing
reader to his own enjoyment before he left school, after every trick had been
played, every trap sprung, came my final distressed cry from the heart:

'For Heaven's sake, Philip, there must be *something* you will read!'

'Yeah,' he said, showing a grin twice the width of any I had ever seen on
his face, 'there is.'

'Well – what?'

He pulled the book he *would* read from his hip pocket, where it was hidden
by his long bum-warmer, strictly unregulation pullover. The book was a
tatty copy of a paperbacked James Bond.

He liked Bond books, he said – read them 'all the time'. His brother bought them and passed them on. His dad read them too. His mother didn't like them, but didn't mind his reading them. His sister? She didn't go much on reading, except of course what she had to do for her exams. She was at the High, he said, expecting me to understand. She didn't have time to do more than read what she had to read. She was studying Maths and Physics. She was going to be a teacher.

No matter how often or how much we congratulate ourselves on the literacy of our society, on the advances in our education system since it became a system in the 1860's, no matter how much publishers claim to be in the forefront of our export industries, and how often we produce book-sellers' figures to show that we are buying more books, and public library figures to show that we are borrowing more books, the fact remains that 60 per cent of Britain's overcrowded 'literate' population rarely, if ever, buy a book; rarely, if ever, borrow a library book. And of the books that are bought and borrowed, the greater number tend to be what the librarians cannily call 'non-fiction'.

We never see any relevant figures set together: it seems to be a tendency to quote library loan figures for a year without mentioning how many members borrowed the books. The figures are then set against the total population and the figures for the last year and it looks rosy, and rosier year by year. We forget that the English-speaking world is enormous in number, and so when we see publication figures and the publishers' annual makings we don't remember that we live among a population of 50 million in this country alone. Among those 50 million plus, a print figure of 3000 copies – an optimistic first run for both a children's and an adult novel – is a normal and usually accepted part of a publisher's thinking.

Reluctance, we might say, occurs in those who have the ability to read without any mechanical problems but have little or no inclination to read except what is required by way of work or normal everyday life. I put the figure at 60 per cent, realising I have not a hope of establishing this as a scientifically proven fact, and rely on every professional bookman's honest assessment of the people he serves to know that it is a pretty accurate assessment of the situation. I am talking only about the reading of creative litera-ture: novels, stories, poetry and plays.

Reluctance is a psychological disinclination. For a variety of reasons the submerged 60 per cent find the activity of reading novels and the novels themselves unattractive. It is not a manifestation of any one intellectual or social group. There are Cambridge professors who find novels anathema and never touch anything more creative than their daily paper. There are wealthy industrial barons sired by established aristocratic families, who find novels a waste of their time, and think the activity of reading them the pastime of lazy men. Equally, there are back-street city kids, ragged behind and smudged in the face, who devour everything they can lay hands on that has words on it, and love most of all to read a 'good story', and who at school sit through seven dollops of 'education' every school day, labelled 'backward' and 'dull', 'uncultured' and 'under-privileged'.

I have spent a good deal of time – too long – listening and talking in conference rooms where reluctant readers were discussed. Always the same hoary remarks roll out to a varying degree of despair, condescension, or pity:

> Children of 13 and more lose the reading habit.
> There are no books they can enjoy.
> Why must everything they read be of such a poor quality?
> Of course, the best writing is never appreciated except by the very few.
> How can we get them to read?
> They just sit and look at the same words all the time.

On and on. Everyone recognises the problem: everyone from the Backward teacher to the University lecturer in English. Their pupils won't read fiction. They haven't read. What should they read anyway? Should they read? Does it matter anyhow?

The statement of the problem slowly leads to the denunciation, and then to the position 'if they won't join us, let us join them'. Let us proclaim that a New Sensibility is here: the mass media have created new, more exciting, more vital forms of expression! At last, go up the sighs, at last we can let the printed word slip into its 'correct' perspective. After hundreds of years of domination by the printed word we can give up the effort. Let those who will read do so; but let those of us, the many of us, who would rather not, let us be free to feed our imaginations on other forms of expression and communication. And finally comes McLuhan!

Perhaps this is right; perhaps there is a New Sensibility. But perhaps too we ought to explore the reasons why we are, so many of us, reluctant to read creative literature; why so noticeably at the age of adolescence; what the prospects are; how much in fact is read; and whether it is a valid activity no matter what.

Any such exploration must be a personal one. It can only be the result of one man's odyssey into the twilight of the book culture: all he says can only be based on what he discovered for himself, and what others have said and written and offered of their own separate odysseys. There has yet been no carefully controlled and correctly mounted research into the problem. There ought to have been. This in itself is indicative of the state reading and books are in: we are not yet convinced, despite all we say, of their importance to us as people, of their place in our education, of the need to know accurately what is being written and read and why.

Where I have been able to dig out some helpful figures, I quote them: where I have been able to twist someone's arm and have revealed hitherto carefully guarded trade secrets, I indicate that I have some basis for believing what I say other than my own surmises, though sometimes I am not at liberty to quote the details of what was revealed to me, nor the source. The reader has to accept this, and trust it, or leave the rest of this book alone.

Let me begin by making the opening statements simply.

> We are discussing the reading of creative fiction among adolescents between the ages of 11 and 17 or so. These ages 'shade' because some develop faster than others.
> We are discussing those whom I estimate to be 60 per cent of the population at that age who can read with reasonable facility but do not read much fiction of any consequence and seem to have lost the taste for it, if it was ever theirs.
> And we are in this chapter attempting to discover the reasons for their reluctance, and the extent of their reading.

Let me first look at face value at the reasons for not reading creative literature often given by young people themselves and by those who deal with them. And let me attempt to evaluate these as true reasons or mere excuses. Like so many remarks made to explain our actions or failures, there might well be meanings underneath the literal direct sense that need teasing out from what is said by anyone seriously enough determined to understand.

1. *I do not like stories*

But *do* like jokes, hearing pals tell yarns, films (often), TV serials (more often), and occasionally the theatre.

Delight in a story is universal, part of man's make-up. When we are given this as the reason for reluctance we are being palmed off with an excuse that either covers a genuine criticism of the books available (of which more – much more – later) or is felt to be enough to avoid further discussion.

2. *I haven't got the time*

Perhaps the most commonly used excuse for not reading fiction. Given by both young and adult alike; used by adults to excuse the young. It is the most laughable of all. Whoever heard of any child who could not, if he wished, find time to read? Whoever came across a child who could not manipulate his life to do precisely what he wished by way of activity within normal limits of behaviour, if he really cares? I would suggest the same is true of most adults, but this lies without my area of discussion. Certainly it is true that any child who cares to can read a good deal of fiction during the course of a normal week. What is actually being said lies much deeper: this is a cover-up remark, an excuse, a smokescreen hardly worth discussing seriously.

There are, of course, moments – weeks sometimes – when some youngsters find themselves mentally and verbally hard pressed in every way: time, energy, inclination. For example, during the times when they are approaching and sitting public examinations and the weeks before leaving school. There may be genuine reason here for a fall-off in reading. But this needs more careful discussion under the title of exams and school leaving.

3. *Teenage is essentially a time of group activity, not conducive to reading*

Most often this is an adult reason advanced to excuse and justify reluctance. At first sight it appears a plausible, acceptable one. Teenagers do, after all, like to be together, like to be active, like to feel part of the group. And why not? Adolescence is a time of transition: a restless, emotionally upset time of life. It is all the psychologists say it is.

And as it is all the psychologists say it is, it should also be a time of life when more rather than less creative reading is done. For is it not also true that a very important need of the adolescent is solitude? Young people, the psychologists say, experience moments of very strong desire to be on their own, and at such times reading becomes a means of communication with others, the way we contemplate ourselves and others, a means by which we come to realise that we are part of the human race, have the same feelings, needs, thoughts, troubles, joys and sorrows as other people. It is the way by which we can come to terms with what is going on, newly realised, about us and within us. It is the time of life when Literature of Recognition is the most meaningful of all art forms. The novel can, as D. H. Lawrence pointed out, 'teach us to live as nothing else can'.

We need not look very far for evidence that all this is so. Looking back on our own reading history, more often than not we find we read most avidly and with most absorption, not when we were very young, but when we were adolescent. Look at the reading histories of so many historical figures and we find again constant reference to the 'long hours' of reading during their teens. (Were they 'long hours', or were they merely remembered in such a way? Whatever is so, they must be an essential part of experience of life at that time to be remembered with such warmth.)

Someone, I know, will charge me with blindness. These people, he will say, were all literary people anyway: they would have liked books no matter what. Reading for them was like football, and fishing, and clothes, and stamp collecting for other people: this happened to be their taste, and because it was their taste, writing became so too, and therefore one is bound to read a lot about people who read a lot as teenagers; and by the same token hear little or nothing about those who read not a word in those long youthful days. Perhaps. I think otherwise.

Merely let me reinforce the point that no matter how gregarious and socially minded teenagers are (when are children not so?) they are still alone a good deal of their time, and have needs often most easily and effectively met through creative fiction.

4. TV and films take up the time given in by-gone days to books and kill the reading habit

An adult reason; one rarely voiced by the young. It does seem an obvious one. But again there are illogicalities. First, the peak time for reading of all kinds, the 8 to 12 years of age, are also the peak TV viewing ages among children and young people. After that time the general indications are that teenagers watch far less than they did as younger children, and less than teenagers did when TV was a novel, emergent media a few years ago. Somehow the 8–12's cram in a good deal of both. If one is to believe those who cry out about reading fall-off, the teens exist on far less of both. And no doubt, many of the reasons already explored are given for the fall-off in TV watching! It all seems to be revolving around what the teenager really does do with his time. If one considers film-going a strong influence, then one also has to remember that it takes up no more than the one or possibly two nights in the week which actually seem to be normal for most adolescents.

Secondly, one also has to account for the effect of TV and film watching on book sales: either shop sales or library borrowings. 'The book' of a popular film or TV show almost always achieves runaway sales. *Mary Poppins*, *The Hundred and One Dalmatians*, *The Sound of Music* and the James Bond Saga are a few of the many. Here TV and film have actually stimulated reading activity. In fact, far from being opposing media, mutually exclusive, I would suggest they have a happily linked relationship; they ought not to be looked upon nor taught to be *opposing* activities, opposing forms of expression, but to be *different* activities, different forms of expression, each with its own areas of appeal and each supplying human cultural needs. They all have their own place, ought all to be engaged in, ought all to be used. There is nothing more despicable and culturally snobbish than the denunciation that goes on, especially among school teachers, about the ill effects of TV, the disabling effect of film watching, and the dangers of both in relation to books. I would certainly argue that imaginative experience based on the written creative word is the best and highest form of such activity, but I would never argue that an exclusive place should be held by any one of them.

These are the superficial, largely meaningless excuses made for reluctance. The real reasons are far more distressing and far less easy to remedy.

Fiction reading is a 'high' form of culture. By this I mean that it requires a good deal of effort and time spent acquiring the ability to read fluently; that it is an activity which relies more on the willingness of the individual to engage in it than any other art form, and therefore needs a good deal of motivation; that it depends on individual choice out of individual taste, which in themselves imply critical selection, and opportunity. It is essentially a private, personal activity that needs time, and circumstances which encourage it.

When we meet reluctance in the teenager, a good deal of this willing response has been heavily damaged or at least disabled. The energy – mental, physical and imaginative energy – which is needed has been neutralised, and this disarmament is the root cause of reluctance. By my definition it cannot be simply mechanical reading failure, and I hope I have shown that it is not the result of the evasive excuses often given for reluctance. What are these root causes? From what do they stem? If we discern this, we can begin to seek ways of rehabilitation and prevention.

Unfortunately the reasons are many and strike deep. Because fiction reading is such a personal matter, the reasons differ with the person. But I hope I can cover most of the general causes, any one or more of which might be the root cause of any one individual's reluctance.

Reading is something that begins, like Charity, at home, and it begins – or should begin – early in life. We ought first to meet the imaginative creative word on the lips of our guardians, no matter who they are. Being told stories from our very early days is of prime importance in the future development of any person as a reader, and especially as a creative reader. Story-telling is done less and less by young mothers at home; more and more children meet the spoken story only when they have started school, or on TV programmes for very young children. Thank goodness there are still strongholds where more than official obeisance is paid to the importance of story-telling! But this does bring us at once to another problem and cause of reluctance.

Ernest Roe in *Teachers, Librarians and Children* (Crosby, Lockwood & Son, 1965), a controversial but stimulating book, makes the point:

> [the] effects of reading – being read to – are intangible and extremely difficult to measure. But the line of argument runs thus: . . . if good books do something towards increasing [children's] understanding of their environment, stimulate intellectual and emotional growth, convey sound values, then contact with them is as important at the age of 2 as at 12, or 20 or 80. Some would maintain that the early contacts are the most vital of all. . . . It may be that the older the child, the more difficult it is for libraries to *begin* to be prominent in his education; or, to put it more positively, that pleasant contact with them in pre-school years facilitates further such contact in primary school years, which in turn facilitates library experience during adolescence. Librarians or library-minded teachers may be seriously handicapped because of gaps in a child's previous experience. (p. 66.)

It is Roe's last sentence which I would like to reinforce strongly. Roe speaks about 'libraries'. It would be no less true if every mention of 'libraries' was replaced by 'books'. It is, I am sure, true and my own personal and teaching experiences support this, that many readers are reluctant because of their lack of early experience with fiction. Reluctant readers are often, as in the case of Philip, reluctant only about certain areas of literature, or, to put it more correctly, are avid readers of only certain kinds of books. I have met adolescents who would read avidly, given the 'right' book, but who could not manage anything that had its roots in say fantasy, or historical fiction. I wonder why? I think part of the answer is that their reading experience at the ages when such stories are most suitable (during their early years in the case of fantasy and during their later primary school years in the case of historical fiction) was deficient: they have a gap in their development. They did not then hear read the Aesop fables, and the Brer Rabbit tales; or they did not read the Greek and Roman myths, the Treece books and so on. Yes, they met the modern Robin Hood. They met him in their comics and the pulp-paper versions. And so they moved more readily to Biggles and Bond to whom the comic Robin is directly related than to Sutcliff and Garner. Though there would be lapses and rebellions no matter what, I am sure that there would be a much reduced problem of reluctance if the work that should be done in the early years were done effectively, and if that homework were steadily built upon throughout the child's school life.

Basically the pattern is simple: a constant quantity of oral retellings plus the opportunity to meet books in every situation, without any fuss or compulsion. Which brings us back home. Telling stories to the children is not engaged in as a daily activity by many parents; and this damage is made ruin because so many homes are without books of any sort, leave alone a goodly supply lying about the place.

Perhaps we would not be much better off if this was so! The architecture of modern houses, open-planned, and difficult to close off into quiet, comfortably personal areas, makes it even more difficult to engage in the activity of reading. It is not true that children need absolute silence in which to read, especially imaginative fiction – they often seem to thrive on some sort of background noise – but it is nevertheless true that in homes where reading must be done in the middle of a lot of family *movement*, concentration is difficult and distraction at its maximum. Naturally, too, where the planning of a home requires that the TV set is, if not visible, then certainly audible to a distracting degree in all the living spaces, even the most avid reader will give up every attempt to prefer the printed word to the TV set, because the electronic picture image is more immediately compelling than a book, and the electronic sound of a TV receiver mentally obliterative. This is when TV and reading do come into opposition: when it is not a matter of choice but of imposition. You have *got* to sit under its influence: the bedrooms are out of bounds or cold, and sitting there in the open-planned living space you cannot *help* hearing and seeing to the exclusion of the written word. Often the child would prefer to read than watch; but the situation is such that he has little option but to watch if he is to keep the peace, or he can make the effort and put up with the bother of a great fuss. He cannot be blamed for staying put and accepting what the architects and his parents have imposed. And slowly his taste for books dies by suffocation, and he becomes one more of those whom we tritely label 'reluctant': a problem and a worry. This is not reluctance, it is the slow murder of a natural response. Sadly, in most cases our reluctant reader and his parents are blissfully unaware of what has happened.

Where there is such blissful ignorance in the home, the worst that 'education' can do often reinforces what has gone on in the family. On the one hand we have a book-ridden education system, while yet on the other a system which pays only lip service to the really vital nature of creative fiction.

Despite the advantages of school TV programmes, film strips, records, tape-recorders and 16-mm films often available freely or very cheaply, the great majority of subject teaching in schools still goes on through the textbook, that dreary, weary, kill-joy weapon beloved of teachers and educational publishers alike. The command, 'turn-to-page-38-and-do-the-first-9-exercises' is very little less prevalent as a teaching method than it was when George Sampson questioned it in 1921 when *English for the English* was first published, than it was when A. E. Smith parodied it in *English in the Modern School*, first published in 1954, and since David Holbrook wrote *English for Maturity*, published in 1961. Every one of these alive men puts forward graphic practical alternatives to this misuse of the printed word in English teaching especially, and in subject teaching generally. All we seem to have achieved is a greater variety of textbooks more colourfully produced. I am not over grateful for that 'advance', for the textbook by its very nature becomes the burden of the desk-bound child, and thus, by blood brotherhood, all books (to change the metaphor) are tarred with the same brush in the child mind.

One finds oneself in the rather odd and apparently illogical position of asking that books be left alone, in a book that asks that books should be more used! It is all a matter of the best tools by which to do a job. Books are not necessarily the best tools by which to teach science, geography, maths or even English. There is often better material, more alive, more meaningful to the child. By placing the burden of the work on books we have created a situation in which children have their noses stuck in books for most of their working day. Naturally they react against them, not just in school but during their leisure time too. Naturally when we come to present them with a choice of fiction books which we want them to read in their own, or even in school time, they prefer not to make the choice. Naturally when we say this is reading which they should enjoy, they laugh hollowly and ask how anyone enjoys something which for most of the working day is considered a chore. Naturally they are very reluctant. We would not expect a navvy who digs drains all day to begin again to dig drains in the evening at home. Rather, to put it mildly, we would consider him over-enthusiastic if he did.

An essential ingredient in the enjoyment of a book of fiction is the sense of relief and relaxed anticipation one brings to it. Ideally, it is with eagerness that we take the book off the shelf, not with a sense of self-imposed or teacher-imposed compulsion. Books admittedly have a 'total' effect on those of us who are 'caught' by them. We don't mind how long or when so long as we have a book. But we are not talking about people in such a state, nor ever likely to be. We are talking about sane mortals for whom the reading of fiction could be and should be a regular part of their lives; people who are not 'book worms' and whom we wouldn't want to be, but whom we would want to discover the enjoyment, the value, and the real importance of creative literature in their growth and understanding of the world and themselves as well as in their relaxation and entertainment. Most reluctant readers are also book-besotted readers. They have words in books thrust at them every school day, and by the time school is over and they have begun a job in which a book is a rare thing that seldom crosses their path, the damage is done and the activity of reading gladly finished with; just as school discipline and manners, school dinners and games, school lessons and all the paraphernalia of exercise books and defaced rulers, satchels, P.E. equipment, and prefects are done with. Maybe they did enjoy them at the time, maybe they look back with some nostalgia, even those who had the hardest passage through. But they know too that they are done with them. And books get a front-line place in that list of by-gones.

The use of books as teaching machines by every teacher of every subject without thought as to whether a book is the best instrument by which to do the job in hand has helped us to a situation in which books are disliked, considered wearisome, and by which we have what we now despairingly call 'reluctant readers'.

In the classroom during English lessons, much more goes on towards the creation of reluctance. An examination system which requires close study of

totally unsuitable fiction must bear a good deal of the blame. The activity of
the specialist who enjoys the analytical approach to literature, and has been
carefully trained in it, is applied in many schools, grammar schools especially,
with fierce rigour on people who will never benefit from such education,
because they have no wish to be literary analysts and because they have no
mind for such work. So, drearily, they sit through lesson after lesson listening
to artificial discussion about what Shakespeare meant or didn't mean in a
particular phrase, how Wordsworth built such sonorous and skilful lines,
and why *Lord of the Flies* must be read allegorically. These are all exciting
things, relevant things, but not, nor necessarily, to all who sit the day
through, measuring the hours by the hardness of a desk seat. Would some of
those same literary analysts want to sit through similar lessons about the
foreign policy of outer Mongolia or the cerebral excitations of the common
field mouse? Both are just as fascinating and relevant *to some minds* as those
literary questions. Had this happened to me at school, I'd have been as
reluctant a politician or biologist as so many others are reluctant readers.
Perhaps it is not remarkable that English students arrive at England's best and
oldest universities, to say nothing of her red-brick and shining aluminium
ones, having read nothing outside their 'O' and 'A' level syllabus, and not
wanting to. One wonders how they have survived as English students at all.
And one sees that those who do read widely in creative fiction often do so
despite their 'education', and not because of it.

Whether one agrees with this extreme position or not, it is certainly true
that examination work tends to exclude reading other than that required by
the syllabus. It does so because human nature is like that and because of the
wearisome bulk of the required exam texts. When one considers the amount
of required reading a History student has to cope with, and equally nowadays the student scientist, if he is conscientious, one is not greatly surprised
that good examination students are also very often reluctant readers of fiction: they too, perhaps more than any other section of the school population,
have been book-besotted, because books are the instruments used in their
education, rather than other tools by which the same information and
stimulus can be given.

There are, in fact, two critical points here: that we misuse books when we
could better be using other means of communication and stimuli; and that
we study creative literature itself in a rigorous system of close, analytical study
first, rather than creating a passion for creative literature which would lead

to a desire to look more closely. After such abuse reluctance is, for most people, the inevitable end.

The C.S.E. examinations in the secondary schools began with a conscious sensitivity to such dangers, but despite initial warnings and attempts to create an examination which would be far more an encouragement to reading than an analytic exercise, the one factor that could not be legislated for is, one suspects, likely to frustrate the good intentions: teachers are human, and being human they tend to follow what was done to them in school; being human they tend to prefer factual, planned, analytic work rather than responsive, imaginative, creative teaching. What was done to them in school were those same things we have discussed and so they tend to perpetuate these techniques in their own teaching. And analytic, factual teaching within a strict framework of a few well-known texts is not only easier, it is safer in exam results, less wearing on the teacher's mind and energy. It is, in fact, a far more secure situation. And security is a human desire. Whether we could ever design an examination which encouraged rather than discouraged creative reading, I don't know. Even if we could, the amount of retraining, indeed reconditioning, necessary to provide teachers capable of using it well would prevent its being implemented.

This is to reach away from my theme: I mean only to make it clear that the present use of books in school militates against their being thought of as anything exciting and desirable by more than the minority; that reluctance, far from being a puzzling problem, is one we should expect as a result of our educational methods. It is not an unredeemable situation; it is not one totally without hope. Many schools contain men and women very awake to these difficulties and abuses, who do fine work in rehabilitating and rejuvenating their own schools and books in them. But there is much to do, and some of the things that might be done are discussed later.

If one is not totally depressed by such things as I have mourned, then one might hope that away from home, away from school, when the adolescent has broken the apron strings and left behind the magistral command, then, free to choose for himself, and with a more genuine choice open to him, he might be encouraged to read again willingly and with enjoyment.

It could be so. Sometimes it is so. But there are depressing indications that it is not very often so. If we were talking about why young people smoke so much, not only would we find just the opposite things being said from the things we have been saying, we could also say:

There are cigarette advertisements on every street corner and public place, in every magazine, paper and bus; in fact, in most places you care to look.

Cigarettes can be bought at tobacconists, sweet shops, grocery stores, Woolworth's and the chain stores generally, garages, public houses, cafés, cinemas, dance-halls, youth clubs, newspaper shops, at any public transport depot, and (if all else fails) from slot machines fairly frequently encountered.

It is socially acceptable to smoke, despite all the publicity against it.

Despite all the Chancellor has done to make them expensive, cigarettes remain within the scope of most teenagers' pockets.

Let us approach books in the same way.

Books are advertised in book trade journals, the 'better' Sunday papers, and in a few of the glossy magazines. There are rarely book adverts anywhere else.

Books can be bought at bookshops (usually found only in the bigger towns, if one doesn't count the inevitable W. H. Smith's which I class as a newsagent).

In *paperback*, a small range will be found in many newsagents and in some sweet and tobacconists' shops though not by any means in all. There have been half-hearted attempts to make outlets in Woolworth's and the similar chain stores, and even via cornflake packets. None have ever provided much choice or any great range, nor been given publicity emphasis.

It is socially not done to read anything but certain popular titles, such as 'the book of the film'.

Though hard-back books have gone up in price less dramatically than any other product, and are, considering the work entailed in producing them, remarkably cheap, and cheaper in this country than most others, they are considered too expensive to buy unless of a 'useful' reference kind.

Paperback books are ridiculously inexpensive and well within the means of every working teenager, and most who are still at school.

One hardly dare point the moral. The 'ethos', the very atmosphere of books in Britain is one of condemnation and a 'fringe' activity. Certainly, such a presentation of books when placed alongside the many other competitive commercial demands for our attention is not likely to encourage a reluctant reader to look to books as a new and exciting way of entertaining himself cheaply.

Just as there is a failure to present books as worth buying, as socially acceptable, as exciting, necessary ancillaries to good and happy living, so there is also a failure to present them as worth borrowing.

The British library service is professionally well staffed, dedicated and hard working. But it is also conservative and curiously unaware of the people who never step over the threshold of a library. Here more than anywhere else one senses the ingrained conviction that only certain people ever can and do read. There is a comfortable 'in' feeling about most public libraries; a rubber-soled air of subdued hush. Many ideas I will later suggest should be old hat to librarians and libraries, yet they are ideas which meet cries of horror and polite noises of denunciation. The fact remains that 60 per cent of the population rarely, if ever, enter a library for any reason at all, let alone to borrow from the banks of plastic-covered novels lining the fiction shelves. While to the teenager, with his natural ebullience, adolescent inability to avoid crashing furniture, or croaking in his half-broken voice, the very atmosphere is repellent. Only in one sector of library work do I notice a widespread and useful mission to the reluctants: in the School Libraries Service of the public libraries. Whenever I have had to do with people responsible for this sector of librarianship, I have found them full of information, desire to help and concern for the children, whom they rarely see personally, and whom they supply with books through the schools. Only they will try most dodges, most titles, every approach the school will allow to meet the reluctant reader with a book he can't put down, and bring more to follow. More and better informed than most teacher-librarians, possessing a knowledge of all sorts of techniques because they are a collect of what goes on in individual schools and libraries, these School Service librarians are in the front line of the attack on reluctance (insofar as there is any movement worthy of being called an attack) and in the encouragement of reading among young people.

Were there to be a sudden and miraculous change, and all these things set right overnight, there would still be reluctant readers. There are certain psychological and social factors involved.

It is a truism that adolescence is an upset time. The two biggest moves occur during this age.

First, the move to the senior school with all it means in acts of initiation; self-consciousness; awareness of the opposite sex and one's own; chafing against authority; disillusionment with the world and often with adults and therefore with all they hold up as sacred or worthy; physical awkwardness; fluctuations of mood; concern about the group and what it considers 'in' and 'out'; serious worries about jobs and the future.

Secondly, the move from school to work. This is perhaps the biggest upset since the beginning of school. We underestimate the disruption it causes in the leaver's life. For some weeks previously, sometimes for his last two terms, it often affects his behaviour, and particularly his ability to concentrate. Adults come nearest to such a time when they are moving house to a new area – abroad perhaps – or making a very important change in their job, and looking at one's own reactions at such times, it is easier to understand why adolescents find absorbed fiction reading difficult, and may often be reluctant to engage in it without a good deal of persuasion and help. On their own such youngsters would not bother at all.

These times can have an effect that appears to be just the opposite: avid reading of the same sort of book. What I call 'the Blyton Neurosis'. We all have favourite sorts of novels. But the mature stable reader will also read other sorts. Some youngsters will read only one type of book, just as many children read only Blyton, or Biggles, or whatever. When one suggests other books, other authors, though they might out of politeness try them, they soon lay them aside, and would rather read nothing other than their 'drug' literature. It seems to me that if such an escape helps the child at that moment, then let him carry on. But it is not the essential activity of creative reading; it is a therapy and may be as much a form of reluctance as any other.

We shall be discussing the available books and the difficulties of finding creative fiction of good quality to satisfy the needs of this age, but we must notice here that this is itself a contributory cause of reluctance. After perhaps 6 or 8 years of fiction reading drawn from a recognisable 'children's literature' (a very wide and varied list of books, enough to supply most tastes for that time, and with a constant flow of new titles on to the market – about 2000 children's books a year and leaving aside at this point critical considerations of these books) the adolescent is faced quite suddenly with a situation in which children's books are now no longer for him, are in fact often anathema, and in which he is lost among the range of adult books (nothing is quite so claustrophobic as standing in front of a strange collection of books), and where there is little that at once provokes a spark of enthusiasm and attracts him, because it is obviously 'his' in the way that children's books are 'theirs'.

So now the wheel has come very nearly full circle. Gaps in reading from earlier ages; the overburdening, suffocating weight of 'school' books and the destructive use of books in school; the commercial impotence of the publisher and bookseller; the psychological and social upsets of adolescence; the critical lack of material tuned to adolescent needs: it is surprising when stated in such terms that anyone survives, that anyone becomes an avid, mature reader. And, of course, to make the point again, only 40 per cent do survive, and of that 40 per cent, one wonders how many are avid readers of creative fiction. It is even wondrous that the 'submerged 60 per cent' read anything at all. It is to the question of how much they do read and then what they read that we must now come.

2

I Know What I Like

How much the approximately four million young people who fall into our age range actually read, and what they read, is possibly the most speculative question yet unresearched by the commercial or academic world. Obtaining figures that might help is like asking for the bomb secrets of the big powers. The problem is further complicated because the girls and the boys have different habits and tastes to a degree more extreme than at any other time in their lives, and because about 60 per cent of those four million are reluctant readers of creative fiction of any orthodox kind.

My own conviction is that a great deal is read by those four million youngsters, reluctant or not; that when we say they read 'nothing' we really intend to say that they read nothing we care to recognise as profitable, healthy or wise. We mean by 'nothing' to condemn what Winston Churchill called the age of 'gape and gloat, clatter and buzz'. And we prefer to turn an unseeing eye to the very large bulk of material read by adolescents.

Thus we say they read 'nothing' when in fact they read a great deal; we say they read 'trash' when we may never have read for any length of time the material the teens see week after week. We bemoan the lack of literature for them when in fact there is a growing industry providing 'literature' which has ever increasing circulation figures. Far from there being 'no writers who understand the needs of young people, and who write for them' one finds a very large body of professional people who understand them so well and write for them so successfully that they are making the 'teen' magazines a lucrative industry.

I want to explore as closely as I can what the teens read without any form of compulsion other than commercial ones because I have come to believe that this provides the most fruitful ground of study for those who would understand the imaginative needs of young people apart from any considerations of literary, moral, 'cultural' value the material might have – or lack – of itself. I want also, by attempting to suggest how much of this material is absorbed, to show that the reluctant reader is far from reluctant if by that we mean he is unwilling to spend time and effort in the mechanical process of 'reading'.

The most clear indication of the bulk of material absorbed by this age is given by the circulation figures of the various popular teen magazines. I am as sure as one can be without the confirmation of systematic research of a deeper nature than the non-specialist in market research can accumulate, that the reluctants are the majority of the readers of these papers.

I took a survey of the magazines most popular among a group of girls of this age and set against them the circulation figures accredited for 1966. The figures are:

Weeklies:

Jackie	365,000 copies per week
True Romances	247,000
Musical Express	237,000
Valentine	220,000
Petticoat★†	200,000
Fabulous	165,000
Trend†	146,000

Monthlies:

Honey	204,000 copies per month
Rave	174,000

These are not by any means all the available papers.‡ They are the sample mentioned to me on the one day of a fifty-person survey. One must add to them the other available material intended specifically for this age, and also the material intended for younger people, but read by many of these older ones. This is something widespread, just as Blyton *et alia* are read by girls and boys who should have outgrown them years ago. It is the Blyton Neurosis

★ *Petticoat* does not reveal its actual circulation. On application, I was told 'We do not normally divulge this type of information for various reasons but I can tell you that our circulation figures are well in excess of 200,000 copies per issue'. I am grateful that *Petticoat* would tell me this much; but it does serve to illustrate how difficult it is to obtain information relevant to our topic.

† Now linked into one magazine as *Petticoat/Trend*.

‡ *Magazines Teenagers Read*, by Connie Alderson (Pergamon, 1968), contains lists, and is a good analysis of these publications based on systematic study methods.

again, a symptom of arrested development. Among these magazines and comics there are even more striking figures:

Bunty	547,000 copies per week
Lady Penelope	538,000
TV 21	495,000
Diana	366,000
Eagle	210,000

and even:

Look and Learn	229,000

If one allows for 'shading' below and above the age range 13 to 17, then the potential market for the teen magazines must be something like 3,000,000 girls. The readership of books and papers is usually calculated at three times the circulation figure. This gives *Jackie* a readership of 1,095,000 and when one bears in mind the amount of swapping and borrowing that goes on at this age, it must be considerably more than that. Place this against the number of magazines of this type on the market and one sees that even allowing for more than one magazine being read by the same person each week (and it is certainly true that most of the girls who read magazines see more than one), the amount of reading matter absorbed is quite staggering, and far from 'nothing'. One must add to this the daily papers that are in part or more read during the week (*Daily Mirror* being the most popular and with a circulation of 5,200,000; and *Reveille* – 1,200,000) and the women's magazines like *Woman's Own*, *Woman's Realm* and so on, many of which the women's daughters read as a matter of course.

Magazines and papers are, one knows, often merely flipped through, the pictures only being looked at and the greater part of the print matter left unread, yet also it must be said many of the girls one talks to know far more about what is in their magazines, what they have said and what the stories were about, than most adults know of their magazines. The teen magazines like *Petticoat* and *Honey* have succeeded in becoming as acceptable, fashionable and as closely followed as 'discs', 'gear' and the 'with-it' TV and wireless shows. They have succeeded where the rest of the publishing industry has failed. And it is a success not solely to be ascribed to unscrupulous advertising, debased morality and exploitation of adolescent day-dreams. We will come to this further on for closer discussion.

A similar study of teenaged boys' reading is much more difficult, because there is no clearly defined literature for them as there is for girls. They often claim to look at a good deal of comic material – *Fantastic, Terrific, Eagle, Victor* and the like (most of these journals with circulation figures around the half million and again a proliferation of them) while every survey I have ever carried out has brought in a crop of other specialist interest magazine material, concerned with fishing, farming, motor-cycles, yachting, stamps, and the like. Almost every boy has regular contact with such material. We add to this the daily papers (with the *Mirror* again running away with most mentions) and the tale is complete.

Both boys and girls also lay claim to reading a good deal of 'book form' material. The girls invariably mention love stories, and their average consumption seems to be about a book a week. One wonders what they mean until one looks at the thirty-two and sixty-four page, pulp-paper novelettes in such series as *True Love Stories*. Sixpenny worth of the poorest book production on the market. I cannot trace sales figures!

The boys claim a lower rate of consumption – average about three chapters a week! – and name war, science fiction and 'avenjure' as the popular themes. My favourite statement of favourite reading comes from a 13-year-old very reluctant reluctant who wrote 'I have read king artur and the nits of the round table'. King Arthur in most versions inspires a similar response in myself.

For the most part the 'books' are paperbacks, bought, borrowed or loaned and often passed on from Dad, Mum, big sister or brother. This inevitably means that most adolescents are reading a good deal of material intended for the adult market, and this must have bearing upon their tastes, development and history as readers.

If one were to reconstruct a typical week's reading of a 15-year-old girl of very moderate intelligence, it might well look like this:

What newspapers do you read during the week?
Daily Mirror. The local paper. *News of the World.*

What magazines do you read? (Underline the mags. you buy.)
Jackie, Fabulous, Lady Penelope, Woman's Weekly.

What sort of stories in book form do you read and how many a week?
Love stories. Three a week.

How many books do you borrow from the school or public library each week, on average?
One a week from the school.

This was in fact one girl's answer given in a survey which I did many times during 7 years of work in a secondary modern school and it is typical of the vast majority of the answers given by girls of this age and ability. Before we breathe too heavily in despair and disgust, let us look very closely at what this girl reads during her week (and compare it with what we personally read in the same unit of time). It is revealing.

Most striking to me is the intended age-range of the material. She takes in newspapers intended for adults (though whether she reads much more than the jokes, and one or two articles that catch her eye, and looks at the pictures, is something that varies considerably. The children were asked to list only what they would consider they 'read' as opposed to 'looked at', and the point was made carefully and often. This is therefore significant: the girl herself, no matter what we think, believes she 'reads' these papers). Yet in her list of magazines she includes *Lady Penelope*, which I would have thought much too young for this girl – her name was Lyn – yet found her quite happy to say she enjoyed it. This is a constant factor in their lists, and their reaction when tackled is often 'Yes, it *is* young for me, but I enjoy the mag. It's fun. My little sis. has it so I read it too.' It is noticeable in Lyn's case that she is still buying it herself. Alongside this she is 'reading' *Woman's Weekly* which is presumably Mum's mag., and read by Lyn because it is there.

The three love stories were pulp sixpennies of the worst sort, and the book a week from the library was certainly an honest claim, for it checked against her personal record in the school library withdrawal register: she had taken on average a book a week for most of her school career. She had once belonged to the public library but had stopped using it some time ago: I gathered just about the time she came into secondary school. Her reason for this was heart-breaking. She said the school had such a good library, she didn't need to use the public library. When I asked her if, now she was leaving school, she would rejoin the public library, she said, no, she didn't think she would. In such a way can success be turned to failure.

She had read many titles that would be considered 'good'. She also read Blyton until her third year. But apart from that had read all the Joan Tate books, *Fifteen*, *Young Mother*, *The Pit*, *The Boy who was Afraid*, and a number of the Five Star Books.

One might rightly say that this girl's staple diet during her adolescent school life was boy-meets-girl stories, pop, fashion, and 'women's things'. It looks a dreary diet: limited, heavily 'emotional', nauseatingly self-conscious; not at all healthy for a growing girl. In many respects this is true. But before we pontificate let us recognise that this menu is also that of most adults. Romance, women's magazine stuff, and a smattering of the newspapers. Lyn's weekly borrowings from the school library (a factor that will vary depending upon where a girl lives and the quality of her school library) are in fact of better quality than the majority of adults ever see, never mind read once a week.

Admittedly, to an adult of reasonable maturity sustained reading of these girls' magazines and papers leads quickly to manic depression. Most of them are dominated by 'Pop' and 'Pop' people, and advertising, though in most it is no more predominant than in other magazines of whatever quality and appeal, from the Sunday coloureds to the specialist papers like *The Bookseller*. Most of these girls' mags *seem* to be given over to more advertising than most, because so much of the advertising is slanted in the same way, promotes similar goods, uses the same images, appeals – sex mainly – and vocabulary:

'the LEAN and LANK and LOVELY look' . . .;
(then after a close-up in colour of a girl's face)
'there's nothing casual about this offer'.

The intended *double entendre* of so obvious a hue makes for nausea. There may be a concentration of such appeals in the girls' magazines, but similar debased use of language we find in all advertising in all magazines. This is not a sickness of girls' magazines only; and I must add that much of the advertising in the girls' glossies is of a higher quality of production and planning than in many adults' magazines. *Honey* and *Rave* are outstanding for this. It is depressing to me to find *Honey* using thirty pages of adverts before the text begins, three-quarters of every double page in the twenty pages following, and thereafter a good deal of copy space and 'articles' given up to what are in fact no more than adverts for girls' clothes: three-quarter-page colour-photos with a few lines of text which include not only the price of the clothes shown but their manufacturers and market outlets. This is no more than gratuitous advertising. My analysis was made of a sample copy, the June 1967 edition. Hidden in those quarter-page columns is some fiction, and this comprises the majority of the copy space available for genuine journalism. A good deal of the 'factual' journalism is handled in the 'story' manner, and written in story-teller's style, contains dialogue and ends with that 'wrapping-up' note of the popular tale. Personal experiences – inside stories of interviews with Pop men, ad. men, publicity men, clothes men and all the fandango of 'gay', with-it living spread here and there through the editorial space. Most of this space is given over, however, to the 'original' short story and serial. Every girls' magazine has its collection, its pregnant anthology of such fiction material.

The common elements of this material almost achieve the eminence of a mythology. With few symbols left unshattered, with no crime or act unknown, with no human secret to uncover because the sex lesson in school, the newspapers, and the documentary immediacy of television news delivery have made known all these things, teenagers, divested of what would once have constituted a cult in which to grow, now erect their own. Let's look at one of these common factors.

The publicity man. He is a remarkably popular figure. He appears in all sorts of guises: as an advertising agent, a publicity agent (often to a Pop group), or even a literary agent or journalist (it's the same job really from this point of view). He is most often 'young, successful and yet mature'. He possesses a remarkable honest cynicism: he is frankly critical of the fans, whom, he constantly tells us, are duped. This is a fascinating element in the stories that use him, for they are being read by, and this information is being quoted at, the very people being criticised and duped. I'm no psychologist and have no wish to set up as one; most of us could suggest reasons for this mental masochism – it is part of my purpose to do no more than note it. He has, this man, the traditional 'dashing' qualities of the prince-hero: money, intelligence, some power, and a position and way of life his readers envy. It is interesting that it is the man who is the power behind the Pop groups who has become the identification hero, rather than Pop star-heroes themselves. Has it something to do with the fact that so much is revealed to the fans about the stars that fictional story handling of the same material would not be successful? (We never did know how princes washed and ate, nor what they wore in bed or used to make their hair shine in days gone by. We know all this about the real-life Pop star: industry relies on it to persuade us to buy their toys.) Is it that, lingering just on the edge of the frame as we watch news film of the stars jogging, waving, down the aeroplane steps, there is the mysterious, half-smiling figure of their manager, their 'agent', their 'creator'? Is it that Brian Epstein, throughout all the days of Beatle mania, was always more interesting to hear in an interview – the few he gave on the subject – than the Beatles were about themselves? Is it that a publicity agent has no need to play a guitar, or look pretty (or ugly), or sing, or be anything that the stars he manipulates have to be? He needs only the prowess of his own native wit to achieve success through others, and – perhaps! – any of us common mortals could do that. If . . .!

Certainly it is true that whenever one finds a story that attempts to use the Pop star as the centre of the story or which involves a group intimately in the plot, there is a feeling that what one is reading is fake, and it remains unconvincing. Most of the intelligent and successful stories in the magazines avoid this.

At the time of writing, *Rave*, the monthly given over completely to Pop and the fringes of Pop – clothes and such – is running a serial called 'Lloyd Alexander, The Strange Adventures of a Gay Young Man'. (Men storytellers or central figures are surprisingly often used in girls' mags.) Lloyd (note the American flavour to the name) has just managed, the lead-in tells us, to 'hold on to his job at Impact Public Relations'. It goes on, 'His latest undertaking, as a publicity manager to a Pop star, promises to be as nerve-racking as the last'. Then follows a four column, full-page, 1000 word episode which describes how Lloyd is used as a decoy for Pop star Simon Brent and is mobbed by fans. Here is vicarious vicarious entertainment: Lloyd experiences what it is like to be a star surrounded by fans, and we experience it through Lloyd. The unrealities of the incident are thereby dismissed as the result of Lloyd's not being the star anyhow. It is easier to suspend disbelief. And it is technically easier for the writer to hold our interest after the incident: one mobbing we can take and enjoy; more than that, as would inevitably be necessary if Lloyd *were* a star, would become a bore. One can't live for long in fiction on such a limited diet of plot (and there can be no greater denial of the validity of 'star' life than this, for it means that, for these people, living, outside the world of fans and what the stars in their interviews call 'work', is at a premium). When we have read through the incident the author merely reveals Lloyd to the story-fans as a stooge, and Lloyd can live again as himself, going on to other, more varied excitements than Poppery.

Here is Lloyd going through it:

> Quick change of plans, and Brent [the star], with a false moustache and glasses, exited through the front door into a small green van, while I went out the back exit, wearing Brent's crimson cloak and accompanied by two bodyguards and the chauffeur. Don Long [the manager] had decided that I could pass for Brent in the gathering dusk.
>
> In fact I almost passed out for him! Girls arrived from all compass points. They were hanging round my neck, pulling out my hair, snatching at buttons, planting kisses all over me – but it was hopeless. I lost my balance and collapsed under a writhing mass of fanatical dollies.

Somehow the bodyguards extricated me from the seething lattice work of limbs and I tumbled into the car. It was only when it started moving off that I realised I had three dollies for company – somehow they had wormed their way in.

They rumbled him of course! Lloyd is one of the lighter, brighter, more convincing creations from this mould. And, unusually, he is the story-teller centre of the plot. Mostly, as I have said, these are mysterious heroes – men to whom girls are engaged or meet, but rarely enter the story for more than a line or two or a visit to the flat, or she to his office at the most. Lloyd is brasher, needs to 'hang on to' his publicity agent's job, and altogether is a healthier creation with a good deal of potential as a character. At the end of this episode, for example, dishevelled and somewhat exhausted after a further drubbing from the fans who caught up with him and rumbled his disguise at the theatre, Lloyd is met by Sue, his assistant:

> 'I was a decoy for Simon Brent', I explained bitterly . . . 'I'm ruined for life.'
> Sue gave me a consoling kiss, and a few sympathetic words and then whispered, 'Do you mean Simon's here at the theatre already?'
> I nodded.
> 'Be a darling, Lloyd, and take me to his dressing room – I *must* get his autograph.'
> 'Oh no – not you too!' I screamed, and walked away slowly, muttering.
> (*Rave*, p. 68, June 1967.)

This is far from the over-sentimental, heart-searching, emotional wallowing so often associated with girls' magazine stories. It is a quality of writing that many children's authors of some standing could not match. It is professional, easy, concise, not at all limited in the way people often expect.

Apart from a wider vocabulary than many people would credit *Rave*'s readers with sufficient ability to manage, there are moments when Lloyd's creator (un-named by the way) touches more than mediocrity in his phrases. Look at this as an example of concise clarity in the description of a typical Pop figure: 'There was a sort of striking collision in his face between innocence in need of protection and dissoluteness in need of correction.'

It is perhaps over-slick ('protection', 'correction') as Lloyd's style often is, but it catches the Pop figures exactly – Presley is precisely this, and is one of the enduring figures in this ephemeral trend world. Neither is it exactly a moronic sentence in the choice of its vocabulary, or its construction. Compare Lloyd's description of a Pop idol, with the ineffective introduction to the Pop group, called the Tykes, on page 16 of John Rowe Townsend's *Hallersage Sound*, a book praised by one reviewer for its 'insight' into the Pop world. Townsend mentions such features as a thin handsome face, brightly coloured spectacles, and thick fair hair, diagonally parted. Maybe there is more detail in Townsend's description, yet I have a less clear picture of his Tykes than of Lloyd's Brent. Townsend has a book of words available, there is no need to be mean; Lloyd's author only about 1000. Yet even when Townsend introduces one of the Tykes on his own later, he mentions only the inevitable 'fair hair' which falls over his forehead, and notes that the girl of the story, Ryl, thinks it can't be dyed.

This is an imaginative failure on Townsend's part. I would suggest that, like so many of the children's authors who try to write a story using the popular hero figure – the Pop groups – in an attempt to appeal to the young and to broaden their readership, as well perhaps in a genuine desire to absorb realities totally ignored by many other writers for the young, Townsend makes one fatal error of creative thinking. And it is thrown into relief by Lloyd Alexander. Only in the comic strip stories of *Valentine* and *Romeo* and the like are groups used as central figures; and whenever they are used in a story as central, as in the Lloyd episode just quoted, they are often looked at with critical sharpness surprising in its clarity. Townsend commits the first error. His Tykes just do not convince me, nor many of the youngsters I've heard talk about the book. In his effort to use the Tykes sympathetically, to avoid making of them either villains of debasement or the real heroes of the book (roles allotted elsewhere), he presents a blurred image. He is neither critical of them, nor able to handle them with sufficient reality, nor, it becomes obvious, does he really worship them in the way many of the young worship their Pop favourites (it would be sad if he did). Young people in their reading detect such things. They react to the imaginative failure, and I would be with them in preferring the liveliness of Lloyd, despite his brash slickness, his quasi-American style, to the aridity of the Townsend creations. Perhaps this is why they are more reluctant to read *Hallersage Sound* than they are to read *Rave*.

I'm not attempting to hold up Lloyd Alexander as a finer piece of work than Townsend's, nor as a literary masterpiece. It is flawed in many ways and has not half the creative force of Townsend's *Gumble's Yard*. What I am saying is that Lloyd is a finer creation and a better piece of writing than such magazines as *Rave* are thought to present, that his implied criticism of 'dollies' and 'Pop' stars is forceful and honest, balanced and mature – adult in fact – and that this is entirely healthy. And most of all I am saying that in Lloyd we see many lessons to be learned by those of us who would aspire to write good teenage fiction that leaves the reluctant as unreluctant as *Rave* does.

All the other symbols of the cult are generally present: cars, restaurants, flats, trips abroad. This framework has taken over from the old symbol of servants, the peerage, high-born romance. And how preferable I find it. This, for example, is one of the hang-over stories from that past glass-slipper age, still extant in *True Love Stories* at 6*d.*, and titled *Summer Dream*. Its author is Gordon Carew, and the print production is of the cheapest in every way. Here is its opening:

> Anthea Bennett felt happy and excited as she popped the last-minute oddments into her suitcase and locked it.
> How lucky she was, she told herself for the hundredth time, to be going to Italy for two long, glorious months! To be travelling first-class too, and staying as a guest in a luxurious villa overlooking the Bay of Naples!
> Anthea was employed as assistant matron in an exclusive finishing school for girls on the outskirts of London. One of the pupils was Rosamund Wynham, whose parents were dead, and who had been adopted by her godmother – an Englishwoman who had married a wealthy Italian nobleman.

Such imaginative anaemia would be better off the market. Placed against this, gay young-man Lloyd becomes a paragon of virtue: he at least can see through the Pop star image and fan world. Mr. Carew and Anthea cannot see through the shallowness of the 'exclusive finishing school', the 'two glorious months', the device of the dead parents (how difficult story-tellers find parents) and finally the debased, decadent image of 'a wealthy Italian nobleman'. Nowhere is the weakness of the creative energy of this insipid story more surely revealed than in its last paragraphs. Indeed it is, generally speaking, a very good test of any literature to look closely at its beginning and end. It is a field yet awaiting a critical study that might well be revealing, and, as the most important moments in any tale, it is needed. The opening engages the reader's attention and the ending fixes the totality of the book in the mind's eye and leaves a lingering image. Remember that brilliant finish to Orwell's *Animal Farm*, in which the disillusioned, disinherited animals peer through the farmhouse window at the pigs' party, and cannot tell the difference between the pigs and the men?

Summer Dream offers this:

> Next moment Hugh's arms were round her, and Anthea's happiness was complete. There was deep gratitude in her heart for Colin's generous gesture.
> 'And – and Rosamund?' she murmured presently, smiling up at Hugh.
> 'At this moment, darling, Rosamund is on the 'phone trying to get through to the airport at Rome to contact Ricky Sherman – the man she loves!' Hugh answered, smiling back at her. 'And you and I are going to be married quite soon, aren't we?' he whispered softly, as he pressed his lips to hers.

Hugh, *of course*, is the adopted heir to the Italian wealth.

Compare this with Lloyd's reaction at the end of the episode of the decoy. In *Summer Dream* the energy has slumped into melodrama ('Ricky Sherman – the man she loves!'), to cliché of the worst kind ('and Anthea's happiness was complete'): the flushed face of false romanticism.

If we take these two examples as spanning the range of quality from top to bottom of magazine fiction we will not be far from the mark. Between lies quite as varied a range of quality as there is in the book publishing field of fiction. The themes and characters are more limited. The symbols are always the same. There is a cult, a mythology that binds it all together, and which adult fiction lacks at present, where the mythology is often peculiar to the author, and one must rethink the meaning with each one. Before we see how this blanket cult of teenage magazine fiction affects the reading of adult books, let us explore a little more the quality of the writing.

Petticoat/Trend is probably the most successful, most varied, best supported girls' magazine in this country at present. The short story and serial occupies a prominent place in its layout. In one test copy (that for 20 June 1967) it contains a lead short story as its first article, called 'The Break', which is followed immediately by 'Cragsmoor', a serial, and that immediately by 'Life with Kathie', another serial. *Petticoat/Trend* is not at all angled to one aspect of 'young life', but gives space to a number of articles of an informative kind about all sorts of topics. In this issue is one about Glyndbourne, a review of a book about England (*Seven Other Years* by Audrey Laski), a careers article written to encourage girls who might be late developers, as well as the usual clothes, interview (with casting directors) and cookery material. *Petticoat/Trend* undoubtedly takes its inspiration from the popular women's weeklies.

The first story, 'The Break' by Vicky Martin, is about a girl's moment of decision: should she go off and marry the successful young writer she has met on the Continent and live with him in Spain, or has she a responsibility to stay with her old grandmother and aunt in their respectable suburban home? On the face of it we have the cult symbols: the successful young writer; the life with him in Spain; the heroine's job as a book-cover artist. But the heart of the story, its major theme, is a difficulty many young girls have to cope with: a life with aged relatives; or marriage away from them. The lifting of the setting to upper middle-class society (the suburban home, the novelist boy, the book-jacket-designer heroine) are chosen to achieve the same results as every romance writer looks for in settings and characters of a 'higher station' than his potential audience. It is the thinking behind *Summer Dream*, with its 'wealthy Italian nobleman'. But whereas *Summer Dream* entered into the wishful thinking of the device, making it the centre of attraction (how I wish I could live like that!), Vicky Martin's story merely uses the device to give the real theme, the conflict in the story, romantic overtones attractive to her readers. It is an engagement device. The writer boy-friend is met only in flash-back and there is no dwelling on 'two glorious months' in Spain (or Italy, or anywhere). 'The Break' is seated in common experience. The opening, for example:

> There were three people whom Hilary James loved – her grandmother, her aunt and Peter – and she thought of them all as she walked up the path. She was two days early and they wouldn't be expecting her and she was unhappy and they wouldn't be expecting that either. She slipped her key into the lock, tired after her journey, and remembered one of the games she used to play as a child. One of the terror games.

I find this quite admirable as a concise, attention-catching opener, which also avoids the fakery of the *Summer Dream* kind of imaginative cliché. The introduction of all the characters in that one opening sentence, linked with the idea of Hilary loving them all. Any girl glancing at this sentence knows that here is a story about love – far and away *the* theme at teenage – and the way those parenthetically linked names strike at her, she expects interaction between them. Then flow the questions germinated in her mind. Where has Hilary been? Why is she early? Most of all, why is she unhappy? And the very cleverly used note on which the paragraph ends: the mention of the childhood terror game. Constant reflection back into childhood is common to teenage, in a way it never is during adulthood. Vicky Martin knows her young people, and she is not embarrassed, as I feel so many writers are, to search in the depths of adolescence for the realities of those days.

From that paragraph the story moves on firmly towards the conclusion, towards the decision we know Hilary will have to make. We are allowed at first only a picture of this girl back in a home from which she has grown away, and gradually we fit in the details: of Peter, and Hilary wanting to marry him; of the sense of responsibility Hilary feels toward her old grandmother and her maiden aunt. There is little relief from the strain and tension of the situation, but it avoids claustrophobia, and within such a short story this is bearable – Lawrence, though admittedly a superior talent, maintains emotionally charged situations far longer, as in 'Odour of Chrysanthemums', or 'You Touched Me'. Vicky Martin balances the tale between the revelations by flash-back of Hilary's meeting and falling in love with Peter, and the day spent shopping with her aunt, catching its respectable dullness. We are even taken in by the aunt's story which she tells Hilary when Hilary at last reveals her problem. Aunt Jo once turned down a young airman, who was later killed in a bombing raid. She advises Hilary to choose her writer and leave grandmother and herself to fend for themselves. The end follows swiftly:

> The two women [Grandmother and Aunt Jo] sat in the kitchen and the only sound was the chatter of knitting needles. 'I thought we'd get a letter today', the old woman said.
> Jo smiled tolerantly. 'You can't expect them to write every day, Mother. After all, they are on their honeymoon!'
> 'But they haven't written at all.'
> 'Yes. They wrote a postcard at the beginning of the week. You remember. Peter put a little note at the bottom sending you his love.'
> Jo put down her book and looked at the old woman, noticing how fast she was becoming faded. Like an old flower. Sometimes Jo missed Hilary so much she could hardly think, but she was happy for her. She thought of the lie she had told, the colourful romantic lie. She almost believed it herself as she told it. It had served its purpose like a fable warning against the dangers of crouching inside yourself too deeply. Jo could not help wishing that someone had shown her how to escape from herself when she was young.

Perhaps, like me, others find this last sentence just too openly didactic, too full of moral purpose. Yet without lengthening the end, it would be difficult to avoid such a wrap-up, and we must remember that this is an adult reaction. I'd risk a fair wager that most girls reading the story would find this end far from disagreeable. What I admire throughout the story, and the closing paragraphs demonstrate the quality, is the sureness of touch, the easy flow of the style (which has a few blemishes of rhythm, but nothing disastrous) and a professional arrangement of the plot that is satisfying. Again I make no claims for it as a masterpiece. But I do claim that there is a directness and a truthfulness here that surpass many children's stories, and most of the books 'turned-out' for the 'older' children's market.

These are not qualities to be despised, no matter what defects we find in the material and its comparative standard alongside the Lawrences and Conrads. That argument shifts ground to a discussion of whether or no *any* form of second-rate literature should be given young people. Let's recognise first that work of Vicky Martin's standard deserves as serious consideration as the book published stories of the acceptable coterie. Let's wash out prejudice first.

'Cragsmoor', the serial which follows on the page after 'The Break', is by

Jennette Letton. The same cult symbols are present again: Cragsmoor is a mansion; Charles, the 'hero', a near-successful playwright not without his professional problems; a New York apartment; trans-Atlantic telephone calls. The very first sentence makes my back hairs rise in distaste: 'A moment later [Kate] had ripped the page out of the typewriter and was across the room and down the stairs.'

There follows a 'happening': Kate, Cathy [the heroine] and Charles have an argument. The style is full of loaded, emotive words and phrases. It is 'soul' language gone mad, *Wuthering Heights* in the hands of a remarkably shoddy writer:

> 'Charles!' Kate's voice pinned him where he was. This was not what he had planned. She had ruined it. She had not behaved as he had willed her to behave. She had trespassed . . . she had violated the sanctity of his concealment. Hate burned uppermost now.
> He reached for his brandy glass. The keen, exultant feeling of being knit with fate rose again.

At the end of the episode:

> He moved to the curtains and drew them. He put his hand on the glass of the windows. It was so cold. It cleared his head and set his thoughts to clicking clocklike, orderly and wise.
> He was free now for the things he must do. All that he needed was here at hand. The women in this house were asleep. For all the threat they were to him they might be dead. Now, in this next hour, that tangled snarl of detail could be picked up and the threads extracted and smoothed out. He knew now what he must do in the immediate present and how to do it.

The conscious, impotent searching after effect fails miserably: 'clicking clocklike, orderly and wise' is bathos of an almost hilarious variety. The 'tangled snarl of detail' and the 'threads extracted and smoothed out' even less subtle than most of this melodramatic, hysterical word spinning. There is none of Batman's humour; none of the nightmarish truth of Poe; and it is without the cheap thrill of Dracula.

'Life with Kathy' follows 'Cragsmoor', and is also a serial. It employs the semi-diary form popular in girls' papers. Kathy again involves all the standard symbols: a successful publisher boy-friend; Kit, a smart photographer come up the hard way; expensive flat-life; a total concern with the 'in', snappy life-about-town. The whole thing is a sort of hep *Mrs. Dale's Diary*, with the same appeals and attractions operating at another level. It is neither particularly offensive, nor particularly outstanding, and I wonder just how many followers Kathy has. They must have a deal of stamina or a deep delight in trivia of a fake kind, to stay with her week by week.

Principally, it is a wish-fulfilment attraction as the end perhaps demonstrates:

> Mrs. Stratford, my Literary Agent, rang to ask if I was turning in any more stories – particularly the one I'd been telling Mrs. D. (Fiction Editor) about over lunch.
> Sara was at home – tried the story on her.
> 'I like it', she said doubtfully, 'bit bitter, isn't it?' Have sent it off – all the same.

The pretended ease with things literary: the agent; the expression 'turning in any more stories' (laughably lacking in truth to anyone involved in 'turning in' stories, and the more denigrating to the author of Kathy for that); and the hint of knowledgeable experience of life in Sara's 'a bit bitter isn't it?' Here we have no starry-eyed innocent, no soul-searching author-genius. Intensity of this sort has gone out with the decline of dedication and belief in hard work. Kathy is the smooth, sophisticated woman-about-town who week by week solves the problems of 'the people in Kathy's life', and dashes off a few stories between times.

Within the one magazine we meet almost the whole range of quality to be found in girls' magazines. And *Petticoat/Trend* is one of the better-produced, more genuinely honest of them all. One gains the impression in correspondence with the editorial staff that they really do care about the people who read what they produce. Certainly they go to some lengths to make one feel the personality of their organisation. And this is to be encouraged if nothing else. The pity of it is that young people do not receive the same encouragement, the same involved interest from the publishers of better things than the weekly magazines. For whatever can be said against these papers, we must constantly keep in mind the fact that they command a reading population the rest of us find difficult to reach, and what they print for that market seems to supply a need, and a creative need, no matter how embryonic, how shallow, or how tiresomely limited.

If sustained reading of *Petticoat/Trend*, *Honey* or any of the magazines which include short stories were accompanied by sustained reading of full-length books of fiction of a high quality, I would laugh in the Devil's face, hoot at the pessimists who decry light, escapist reading, and feel no perturbation. Unfortunately, what seems to be so for most girls is that the magazines are the only sustained reading that ever engages them.

The magazines have certain advantages as vehicles by which such material is marketed: they are and have the look of ephemeral forms of print. The Young Adult literature of the United States is a book industry, paperback, but 'book' as well as magazine. And this, I think, is a less healthy situation than in Britain. I would not want to see books full of the run-of-the-mill stories published in our girls' weeklies, which is precisely the American situation. Because magazines are ephemeral, one hopes their effect is not so profound, yet one cannot help supposing that a sustained reading of such literature week after week, unrelieved by any deeper reading experience, is disabling. The mind must become tuned to the telegraphed style, the colourless vocabulary, the clichéd ideas, and the total mythology of the teenage magazine story world. There can be little sensitive exploration of emotion and relationships in the 'short complete' as they are called – stories of about 2000 words – taking up one page or at most a double spread inside the magazine. There can be little because there are not enough writers capable of such a high standard of work: short story writing is the most difficult art to do well of all the fiction forms.

One does indeed often encounter confused purpose in many of these tales. As an example, let me quote from 'The Day I Left the Scene' by Penny Weston, a story of about 2000 words published in *Trend* for 20 May 1967. It is sub-titled 'A Story of a too possessive, pointless love!' We would assume from this that the intention of the story is to point-up the old idea that love between two people must also allow of independence as well as inter-dependence. It is exploiting a common experience, just as 'The Break' does. Most girls or boys go through a relationship in which their partner is over-possessive. Yet the focus of the story slips in the telling, and by the end of the 2000 words, instead of making the point suggested in the sub-title we have something not at all as laudable or proper, but in fact just the opposite.

Julie is engaged to Tommy. One night she goes to a discotheque on her own. Tommy objects to such behaviour and there is an argument during which Julie throws her ring in Tommy's face. Julie later meets old pal Steve, pours out her grievance, goes off to the disc. with him, after which:

> I bumped into a lot of my old friends whom I hadn't seen recently. 'Long time no see', they said, and wondered what I was doing with Steve.
> When Steve drove me home that evening we fell into each other's arms. I felt almost as if we were fated to meet and fall in love.

Tommy was right to object it seems. Some time later, Tommy turns up, offering the ring back, 'But you must promise me you will do as I say from now on.'

More argument:

> 'No, Tommy!' I cried . . . 'You think that as I'm engaged to you that you own me. You've spoilt everything . . . You don't trust me' I said . . .
>
> 'How can I?' he said crossly. 'When you run off with every Tom, Dick and Harry when I let you out of my sight.'
>
> 'You know that's not true,' I said and I heard my voice rise to a screech. 'You've killed our love – love can't exist without trust, Tommy.'

My sympathies are with Tommy, and clearly they are not intended to be. The fact is that engagement does mean just the commitment to one another that Julie is avoiding; that she herself has shown what Tommy says about her is true, that her denials are fake. Maybe this is to treat the entire, ill-written incident too seriously. But I wish to point up the confusion there really is in this story, all the more dangerous because – I presume; I almost hope – Penny Weston does not realise the confusion exists. What she has actually said is that despite an engagement for marriage, it is quite all right to go off behind your fiancé's back and live it up with the kids. And this is not what she intended to imply.

Dick Long in the same week's issue of *Valentine*, on the surface a much less salubrious production than *Trend* (both take their 'inspiration' from Pop), handles something of the same topic very much better. At this time Long had a serial running called 'Tomorrow's gonna be Another Day'. The usual symbols: an actor hero; a would-be actress heroine; casting secretaries; casting directors; and set abroad in Ireland. Long's writing is much more honest, because he is much more interested in his characters than their morals. 'The Day I Left the Scene' began, I'd guess, as an interest in an idea – possessive love. 'Tomorrow's gonna be Another Day' began as a story. Long makes much more of it without in any way labouring things. The hero – Paddy – is an extrovert, dashing, amoral go-getter; the heroine, Mary, is a pretty, well-drawn, ordinary lass. Paddy imposes on her incorrigibly, and the question of personal responsibility and integrity is lightly handled through the episode, which centres round an abandoned baby Paddy dumps on Mary. There are redeeming moments of near farcical comedy, and a humanity about the whole thing much lacking in Penny Weston's moral tale.

I have been waylaid again into a discussion of the relative merits of different stories, but again they help me make the point that though no one likes the idea of our young people reading endless quantities of such ephemeral material, it is also true that there is a surprising amount of a better quality than we often suppose.

A major disability such reading aggravates is that of already weakened stamina; full-length books become less and less attractive, the effort to read them more and more conscious and painful. I am sure this underlies the reluctance many of the magazine readers suffer from in any case but which the brief magazine story intensifies.

And so we see that despite all the qualities many of the stories possess, despite the fact that they are on the whole of a higher quality than similar material before the 1939 war (*Red Letter* and the like), despite the apparent concern felt for their readers by the editorial staffs on the magazines, the total effect is more likely to be disabling than helpful. Unless the reading of such magazines is accompanied by a good deal of more demanding literature.

Let me also say, however, that the magazines have a good many lessons to teach those of us concerned with writing for the young, those of us who must judge what is written for them, and those of us responsible for their reading, though in the final count-up all this is neutralized by the nation of butterfly minds the popular magazines help create when it is the only diet of reading that enters people's lives.

All I have said about the girls' magazines applies to the comics boys tend to look at, only more so. In most directions reading comics is even more disabling than reading the stories we've been discussing, and I have little sympathy for the comic industry which might die tomorrow so far as I'm concerned. It is a reading habit which reaches the level of sickness. One is delighted when boys read comics at speed as they often seem to do, paying no attention to the words, and apparently little to the pictures. At least this way comics are less likely to have an effect. One is even more pleased when the comic 'craze' is over.

Unfortunately for many it never is, as the profusion of comic strips in the popular (and serious) papers gives evidence.

Study of the magazines that boys read – the specialist interest mags, and the papers, as well as the pulp-paper books mostly involved with war, horror and sex – leads to an interesting speculation about how these papers supply boys' creative reading needs. Almost every paper carries a high percentage of articles which are handled in 'story' fashion. These can be about almost anything, even technical processes. But most often they concern personalities or happenings. (Character and plot?) Thus a football star will be written up in a style which goes further than studied biography and becomes almost a fiction. 'Written up' is a phrase current in editorial departments, and it suggests exactly what is done. In other words, I'm suggesting that story journalism for many boys takes the place of truly creative story fiction. The 'non-fiction' war stories, of course, do exactly this too.

Interestingly enough, most of these journalists' 'stories' comprise all the elements of the old romantic hero story: the local boy makes good; the footballer who rose from the back streets by guts, hard-work and pluck to stardom and fame. *If we wanted to*, we feel, we could all rise by guts, and hard work. Luck is something that no one has any control over and so it is an acceptable element in the story, as 'string-pulling', money influence, geography and sociology of birth, attendance at the right school, and so on, are not. Even when these have been the almost obvious means by which a famous person has 'reached the top', journalistic stories are at pains to avoid admitting it.

I labour the point because I think there is a lot in such a study which we can learn about boys' reading, especially when we compare it with the accepted children's books, about which I will say things soon. There remains about such writing as this a frank hero-worship, an appeal to wish-fulfilment which were finely present in the good as well as the indifferent novels of the last century, but which have gone out of our present literature, even children's literature, to a very large degree. Bond is so successful because he appeals to these instincts again. Whether we like them as instincts or not, they are there, common to almost every child that lives, and we are neglecting them to a dangerous extent. One of the most welcome things about Sir Francis Chichester's trip in 1967 was that at last here was a genuine hero of sufficient stature performing an act of great physical and personal courage to whom these instincts could be healthily directed. But Chichesters grow rare, as rare in literature as in life, and the journalist-created semi-real figures of the specialist interest papers, from Pop mags to *Time-Life*, are dangerous because they are souped up from real personalities who usually are not of the stature they are written up to be; and are not genuine fictional creations which can take on an independent life of their own.

Many of the Five Star titles I discuss later and list in Appendix A are successful because they are books which satisfy these two basic instincts: hero-worship, and wish-fulfilment during which a reader explores his own needs, albeit unconsciously.

Is there value in reading this type of literature? Is there value in reading for reading's sake? I think not. Certainly there is no need to encourage children to read comics or magazines – as we've seen, they do this most willingly. But if we imply that therefore reading is no more valuable than any other recreational activity – no more valuable than a rowdy game of soccer, or stamp collecting, or cycling, or what-have-you, then I can't agree. And this is often implied when this same question is put. Creative fiction is a basic element in the growth of a properly working human personality within a culture like ours. It harks back to the story-teller of primitive society, to the aural tradition of man. It has a different nature and a more profound effect than the 'healthy hobby'. It opens the doors of emotional understanding of oneself, other people and the world about one. And all this cannot be gained in quite the same way by any other means. Reading has no value in itself. Reading of a disabling literature will in fact be harmful. But the reading of creative fiction is a necessity to a developed 'civilised' being.

It is like poor food and foul air.

We go on eating poor food because we don't know there is better, or because we were not brought up with the taste for better. We breathe foul air because we have created the foul air, and often because the foul air stretches over such an area of the land that the effort of reaching the fresh air is too demanding. In the end we notice neither the poor food nor the foul air, and may even talk as though we prefer them. Nevertheless, preferring them or not, we go on eating and breathing the inferior harmful stuff because we must eat and breathe: they are functions essential in life. In the same way, verbal experience of life carried on in our imagination is an essential function of social-intellectual-spiritual life and we deny it at our peril.

Therefore the problem remains: teach people to read and most will read willingly. But they willingly read only what they like. Reluctant readers know what they like and they find it in the popular magazines. The magazines merely deepen their reluctance to read more solid work. But also the solid work available seems to have little common ground with the fiction they know they like. This is not just a gap, it is a cultural failure. There are some books which most people responsible for what teenagers read find successful. These I have called Five Star books. Maybe by examining them we can discover something about why they are so generally successful; whether successful books must inevitably be of a poor quality; and perhaps even if there are common themes, characters, treatments – anything – that might indicate the basic elements of good teenage literature.

3

I Couldn't Put It Down

EVERY adult who has to do with young people and their reading has experienced the joy of the moment when a youngster returns a book with that glint of satisfaction in the face and the words 'I couldn't put it down!' It is an accolade of success; it is a moment of warmth and delight in the knowledge of an experience shared. Or again, the sight of another person so involved in the book he is reading that distraction becomes almost impossible and certainly an outrage. There is quite a different atmosphere, quite a different 'look' about a person reading in such a 'deep' way, in contrast with times when they read because it is required; or because they just felt like reading and have a book, any book, but not so compelling as one 'I couldn't put down!'

Certain indications other than 'atmosphere' or 'look' – which depend after all on the observer's sensitivity, not his diagnostic ability – usually accompany deep, involved reading.

1. Reading speed increases considerably, often to a rate surprising even to those who know to look for it

Everyone expert in teaching 'backward' readers knows that with the 'right' book a very poor reader who labours painfully with most texts will be found turning pages at a rate that makes one wonder whether or no he is just pretending to read. After a test, one finds that this story is known better than the ones ploughed through more slowly. It is also a matter of one's own experience, surely? The very day on which I drafted this paragraph I had a manuscript novel to read for a publisher and I began William Golding's *The Pyramid*. The one was forced work and despite my desire to get it off my hands with all honest despatch, I read the work at just a little over half the pace at which I devoured the Golding novel, which was more complicated, verbally more profound; yet was also something looked forward to, very much enjoyed and of a quality way above the manuscript novel. In fact, I couldn't put it down. The manuscript I longed to put down. This sort of thing is common to us all and should cause no surprise when we find it common also to readers more reluctant than ourselves. It is therefore something we should look for in dealing with reluctance.

The surprising thing is that we so often do not. The surprising thing is that we use 'Reluctant Readers': books specially produced by the educational publishers, which have reduced vocabularies, 'with-it' stories, shortened sentences, bigger or wider-spaced letters, fewer lines, more illustrations, and all the devices of those whose professional job it is to remove the reluctance so often, it seems to me, only deepened by such reduced, indeed petrified 'literature'. The devices might for a moment or two inspire some willingness because there is something less difficult about these books than others the victim has had thrust under his nose and been told to 'read from' over the weeks, months or years, but inevitably the devices become as dull or even duller over the weeks, months or years of their use, as the 'less suitable' material they replaced.

Book reading of an absorbed, useful kind, it seems to me, must be – it is its nature to be – of a freely chosen kind, individually selected, and willingly undertaken. Without these conditions any reading of any sort will become, but for the Grace of God, reluctant.

For all their faults, for all their tendency to disable, the girls' magazines and the boys' comics and war books are often read with just this absorbed 'givenness'.

2. *As the reading rate increases, so long, difficult words, phrases and even passages impede less*

No doubt the educational psychologist will nod wryly and say something like 'Naturally! What you'd expect. At greater speed you can take in the sense of whole word structures and guess what individual words and phrases mean.' How surprising then that we pay such little attention to children's ability to cope with whole sentence structures. We give up teaching to read as soon as the child can stammer through the primers that teach him about letter combinations, and forget that the job is only half done: that it is not finished until we can handle word combinations, sentence structures and a book full of paragraphs.

Certainly it is true that great motivation to read a book carries a child through very difficult verbal passages. The Biggles books demonstrate this. Johns' style has a high vocabulary count. He uses some 'hard' words: quite a smattering of them on any random page you like to choose.

> Biggles judged the Count to be a man a little past the middle age; say, between forty-five and fifty. Of average height, he was rather plump, as if he did himself well. His skin without a wrinkle on it was that curious colour, almost a pallor, peculiar to the Eastern Mediterranean, Greece in particular. His hair was beginning to recede from the temples. His clothes were immaculate and obviously expensive. He moved easily. In a word, his general appearance might have been described as sleek; sleek in the manner of a well-fed house cat. But there was nothing objectionable about him, in appearance, manner or the way he spoke. Nevertheless, prejudiced perhaps from an unfortunate experience, the man was a type Biggles would not have trusted too far until he knew him better.

The chapter from which this passage comes is headed 'A Proposition' ('What's a proper what's it?') and is on page 39 of the 76th Biggles book, *Biggles and the Gun Runners*, published in 1966. Johns is an erratic writer. Sometimes his style is distinctly more difficult than this, sometimes very much 'easier', but this random extract serves to show what I mean when I say that absorbed reading covers a multitude of difficulties.

Remembering that Biggles is read now between the ages of 8 and 13 – the less able reluctants come to him between 10 and 13 – for even an 'average' intelligence there are 'difficult' words: pallor, recede, peculiar, immaculate, objectionable, and that cacophonous mystery-making phrase: 'Nevertheless, prejudiced perhaps from an unfortunate experience. . . .' Add to this the complexity of the style, shown even in this short passage ('His skin, without a wrinkle in it, was that curious colour, almost a pallor, peculiar to the Eastern Mediterranean, Greece in particular') and one might well wonder why Johns is so supremely popular among boys of all kinds. The answer lies elsewhere than in his sentence structure or vocabulary, of course. He has the story-teller's basic ability to fit incidents together in such a way that one's curiosity will not let go. By fascinating tit-bits of mysterious information, clues, questions, and conceding the occasional satisfaction of a climax, Johns leads the curiosity on, the reader taking the verbal and stylistic hurdles easily because of the excited pace of the reading. One can't put it down, one can't read it slowly, one is forced irrevocably onwards. And in the end, if a passage proves mystifyingly difficult just skip: it doesn't matter: Johns is the sort of writer who repeats himself, not using the same words but in the way he leads to the moments of 'plot significance', prepares for them and executes them.

There is the feeling of 'I knew this was going to happen' and sometimes the feeling 'but I didn't know it would happen quite like that'. So the difficult words, the complexity of the style are left behind, unnoticed, unheeded, and unnecessary. They are dressing only. Never essentials. It is, in fact, not always a matter of the speed allowing of the comprehension of whole sentences rather than single words, but simply the age-old device of skipping which saves us. (And that depends upon the effect of the skipping on the writer's work. Some books can't be skipped at any point. And often, the better the writer the less one can skip merely to overcome verbal or stylistic difficulties. The writing is too economic to allow it.)

3. *The desire for 'more like this' at the end of the book*

So we get the 'craze' in reading as we get the 'craze' in other activities. We have favourite authors, favourite kinds of books. This is natural to us all and, in the reluctant reader, not only a sign of success, also perhaps, ironically, the moment of defeat.

Publishers know well that series books sell, and children like them. Publishers and children love even more the series author – the writer who can turn out time after time another one like the last. It is justified because it keeps children reading (it also makes publishing much easier, much cheaper, and much more lucrative). To some degree the series titles and authors serve very useful educational purposes, and provide a good deal of entertainment, but when their output amounts to a veritable library of books 'like this one', as supremely in the cases of Blyton, Johns, Crompton, Richards, Buckeridge, and so on, there may be dangers one would prefer not to lay in children's way.

Mankind is a lazy beast, and reluctant readers are by another definition lazy readers. It is just possible that, by serving them with books all alike just because they are sure of success, we are our own worst enemy, and theirs. For, perhaps, they will never leave the series, never find the stamina needed to explore other books, other writers. Most of all, never develop their ability to nose out new books which will excite them. This, more than anything, more than considerations of literary merit, morality, or 'educational value', is the most dangerous aspect of the Blyton Neurosis. Because there are so many 'like the last one' the drug has time to take hold, to hook the victim and ever after, when at last we've read the 78th version of Biggles, the 24th version of the Famous Five, the 34th version of William (though I find him less addictive than the other two), we are unable to find anyone like them to read. Where do we go? What do we look for? After Blyton everything else is so difficult! After Biggles . . .? (Bond, of course! Why didn't we think of it before! Maybe Biggles is more responsible than Ian Fleming for the 45 million copies sold of James Bond stories. There is after all a surprising similarity in technique, style, activity, even central character. Bond, the super Biggles. What a pity it is Mr. Fleming is not here to speak from the horse's mouth about the influence of Biggles on Bond! What a fascinating study it would be! And not so terribly far out either, perhaps.)

Series which include work by many authors are a different matter. These are not only helpful to child, teacher and librarian, they need not be prone to the dangers of one-author series. We tend to forget, because they are now so large and so much an accepted feature of the book landscape, that Penguin Books, Puffin Books, and their later rivals are all series books, at least in conception. In the days of their unrivalled supremacy just after the Second World War, Penguin Books all looked the same, only the title and author lines differing. They made their name as a quality production in this way. As a result many people came to read books which otherwise they would never have met. The same goes for series publishing and the reluctant reader. Naturally such publishing varies in quality. It is a publisher's responsibility and we must be on the watch for the worst that can be done with such a useful form of marketing. But potentially one finds series publishing *of this kind* a welcome thing.

The railroad effect of the bulky series – once on the rails you can't get off: this is the danger of libraries of similar stories, characters and authors. Drug reading – as vicious and dangerous as chemical drugs and with very much the same results: ultimately the death of imagination, the petrifaction of any ability to think outside the mental *mores* of the favourite author and favourite books. If the reluctant reader reads anything and likes it, he wants only more of the same, please, because I know what I like and like what I know. It is a temptation to be resisted, as writers, as publishers, as librarians and as teachers. Perhaps as readers too!

4. *The desire to talk to someone else about a book that has involved us deeply. 'Have you read this? I couldn't put it down'*

Again, naturally something we all experience and shouldn't be surprised when the reluctant reader experiences it too; should be very happy, in fact.

Not only because it is a sign of success – he's read a book with enjoyment and which has meant something to him – but because it is such an opportunity to carry the cure a stage further. Having read a book at this level, one talks about it; having talked about it, the book becomes part of one in a sense it had not before; having become part of one, it has become a natural, a right thing to consider that book in particular and books in general in a different light from before: they become first a natural, a proper, an acceptable part of life; and in the end they become an integral part of life: one of the instruments necessary to the exploration of life. To use the correct terminology, books have become part of our culture. We want them, need them, use them. And we use them then in that unself-conscious, relaxed way which shows they have become part of us. We have become avid readers, though we hope discriminating readers too.

Let us note for the moment this natural response to the experience of a deeply enjoyed book. There are conclusions to be drawn, as there are from each one of these 'tests', these manifestations of the experience in process.

We know that the girls' magazine stories have these same effects on reluctant girls' reading; we know that comics, and the specialist magazines, as well as some war books and other less salubrious pulp books affect the boys like this. But are there books of a better quality, of more laudable merit than these, which also have the same effect on reluctants? There are: the Five Star Books already mentioned, and I want now to examine some of them (not that there are many, and what there are I have listed in the Five Star list in Appendix A).

Fifteen by BEVERLY CLEARY, published by Peacock/Penguin Books.

I can almost hear the groans go up! Every practitioner in the business of young people's books knows this title. We all use it, we all smile as it works its sway almost inevitably on the majority of reluctant readers among the girls (and – though vociferously denied if suggested to them – by reluctant reader boys too). It is the standby, the natural, the first title we think of suggesting. For that very reason it must come first and be dealt with fairly closely. Bear with me.

Fifteen is an American story about one Jane Purdy, 'an ordinary sort of girl' who longs to have her first real date with a boy. She achieves her ambition: she is dated by Stan Crandell, a handsome newcomer to the small town of Woodmont. In the course of the summer Jane copes with her parents, her friends, her rivals, Stan, and herself as her emotions travel the ladder of adolescent love. It is the book above all others I know which exemplifies *at a minor level* what is meant by 'literature of recognition'. In it adolescent girls find many of the things they wonder about themselves set in a story of simple directness that is appealing even to crusty adults. The moment after the book is finished and the reader has past it enthusiastically to her best pal, she is chuckling with amusement at the entire incident. The moment is past, she has grown that step, the book seems somehow so much younger than all of a sudden she feels she is. She has seen herself as she is in Jane Purdy and so become just that little bit older, more adult. (Boys like it, of course, because it is such a gleeful insight into girls.)

It has its faults. 'But, sir – it takes him 174 pages to kiss her!' (There are 175 pages in the book.) Well, yes it does. And, yes, in real life he *would* have done it before then. We have hit the jackpot at once in discovering difficulties in writing for young people: how honest dare one, can one be? How much of what really does go on at that age *should* one include in books intended for them? The problem of truth.

There is also something of an impression given by the end of the book that this first-time date will also be a forever date, and here I feel Beverly Cleary's instincts betray her. All right, so there has to be a happy ending. Yes, the book does need a smooth finish. But it is also true that most first dates are the first of many dates with many boys; that it is generally speaking better so; that to suggest first dates become forever dates for most 'ordinary' girls like Jane Purdy is misleading and – for me – somewhat mars a book which otherwise catches something of the truth of adolescent boy–girl relationships, despite its 'popular' approach.

But the good things. The directness first. Look at the opening paragraph:

> Today I'm going to meet a boy, Jane Purdy told herself, as she walked up Blossom Street toward her baby-sitting job. *Today I'm going to meet a boy.* If she thought it often enough as if she really believed it, maybe she actually would meet a boy even though she was headed for Sandra Norton's house and the worst baby-sitting job in Woodmont.

It just can't fail. The statement of the plot could hardly be more simple, direct, engaging. Of course Jane will meet her boy, as inevitably as Cinderella sweeping the hearth in her ragged clothes will meet the prince. (Jane too is going about a chore, note.) We know it, and we can't wait to read of the moment when it happens. We rush on, reading rate accelerating to top speed, curiosity caught, and eye unimpeded by verbal or syntactic worries. (In the first three pages only 'convertible', 'occasional', 'housing development', 'notorious' would cause any bother at all and these only to the weakest of the readers likely to find the book. Compare this with Biggles, read much earlier in life too.) There is, though, no conscious limitation of the style or verbal choice: to the adolescent reader, the book seems, at the time of reading, adult. Certainly (another advantage considering the majority of the audience likely to read *Fifteen*) the opening has more in common with the magazine stories than the books most likely to have been put in front of young people in school. And, indeed, the book does have a lot in common with the magazine fiction we discussed earlier. The boy–girl story. The theme: just be your confident self and you'll win through. The directness of the style. The un-embarrassed way adolescent behaviour is handled (things like dreamy moping on one's bed, long telephone calls and the agony of waiting for them, the wavering decision–indecision, and the flustered moments of shyness: all things adults find distasteful to dwell on, even to remember, and commonly find irritating to endure). These things are all far more common to the magazine writers than the accepted fiction writers for the young. Consider this, for example:

> Mrs. Purdy went on in a voice so low Jane had to strain to catch her words. 'I'm glad our daughter is a sweet, sensible girl'.
> Mom, how could you, thought Jane. Sweet and *sensible* – how perfectly awful. Nobody wanted to be sweet and sensible, at least not a girl in high school. Jane hoped her mother would not spread it around Woodmont that she thought her daughter was sweet and sensible. The telephone rang so unexpectedly that she jumped before she was able to pick up the receiver. 'Hello', she said almost absent-mindedly, because her thoughts had drifted back to the strange boy who had smiled at her across the Norton's kitchen.
> 'Uh . . . is this Jane Purdy?' asked a voice – a boy's voice.
> An electric feeling flashed through Jane clear to her finger tips. The boy! It was *his* voice! (p. 30.)

We may not like this, it is certainly not great literature, but it catches the behaviour and thinking of an adolescent girl, does it in competently handled English, and – important this – in a way that strikes a peal of recognition and sympathy in the audience it is intended to reach. Yet it has the 'tone' of magazine story rather than a 'children's book'. This is what makes it such a 'cinch of a book'. More yet: it transcends the magazine story in a number of ways.

First of all, it does so by a clever use of comedy to prevent the dangerous moments taking over – the love scenes are always broken up by comic action, making it possible to control these moments without their being explored more deeply than Beverly Cleary wishes and yet avoiding the sensation that the reader has been duped, that the book is avoiding these moments because they are 'difficult' or 'delicate'. Naturally an adolescent girl wants to read about the moments of love-making, as much as boys want to read about bloodthirsty moments in battle (and moments of love-making). To divert attention by the use of comedy is much the best way out: laughter is as satisfying as pondering the stages of love-making; and it is in itself valuable that adolescent girls should come to see the comic side of such behaviour. No story I have read in the Pop girls' mags has ever used comedy to the same conscious end. The better stories do often involve comic scenes, as I have pointed out, but none of them in my experience has the control and technical purpose of Beverly Cleary's use of comedy.

Here she is, applying the fresh air of laughter at one of these potentially 'romantic' moments:

> 'Come on, Jane,' whispered Stan. 'Let's not sit at the tables with the others. Let's go over by the stream.'
> Jane's smile was her answer. Now she knew that Stan wanted to be alone with her as much as she wanted to be alone with him. Carrying their paper plates of food, they walked through the carpet of wood sorrel that grew along the bank of the stream and found two rocks near the trickle of water. It was a perfect spot to be with Stan. There was a full moon rising through the bay trees. Jane sat down on her rock with a sigh of pleasure. It was a beautiful moonlit night. Perhaps after Stan had eaten his steak he would turn to her and look deep into her eyes . . .
> 'This stream doesn't have much water in it, but at least it's wet,' observed Stan, settling himself on his rock.
> 'It's the only stream I know of round here that has any water at all this time of year,' said Jane, as she eyed her steak. It was large and thin and overhung the edges of the paper plate . . .
> . . . Here goes, thought Jane and sawed at her steak with her cafeteria knife. Nothing happened to the steak, but the pressure of the knife bent the paper plate. Gingerly she tried another side of the steak. This time she succeeded in separating a morsel of meat, which she put into her mouth. That was her mistake. (pp. 165–6.)

The stage is set. We can see what is going to happen, and we are smiling already. Beverly Cleary is not yet ready for Jane and Stan to fall into each other's arms. And in terms of the plot, if not in reality, she is right. So Jane and Stan are made to see the humour of the situation along with us:

> . . . [Jane] attacked her steak once more. As she sawed away, she glanced at Stan to see how he was managing and found him watching to see how she was cutting her meat. All at once the humour of the situation struck Jane and she began to giggle.
> Stan relaxed and laughed, 'Why don't we just pick it up and gnaw?' he suggested. (pp. 166–7.)

It is an amusing, normal, human situation which arises naturally as a result of the plot. There is no contriving to manage it, no straining to avoid the lover's clinch. Before the steak is finished and Stan can really do any eye-gazing, Buzz, the comic extrovert of the story, bounces in with a '*There* you are!' It is Buzz not Beverly Cleary who receives the groans of irritation from the adolescent girl reader who hopes that now at last 'things will happen'.

The heart of this book, rather than the dating of Stan, is the less obtrusive theme of the story. Jane, nervous, shy, ordinary Jane, who begins by thinking that the right way to succeed is by imitating Marcy, the town's vamp, comes to realise that Marcy is one big fake, that the right way to succeed is by being oneself, and as confidently and firmly as can be. There is nothing profound or original about this theme, but there is a good deal to be learned from the way Beverly Cleary handles it by most would-be authors for young people and those of us concerned about standards by which to judge their books. It never obtrudes, is never pushed at us, never served up raw on the paper plate of her book. It is the undercurrent to the plot, the essential acquisition if Jane is to be successful and win Stan. That it is the major theme in the writer's mind is clear. She expends the best written and most satisfying scene in the book on the demonstration of it: Chapter 10, the penultimate chapter of the book, in which Jane decides to buy flowers for Stan, who is in hospital with an acute appendicitis. In the decision to do this, in what flowers to get, in buying them, and most of all in the procession through the main street with a huge bunch of blooms, during which she must run the gauntlet of Marcy and the boys, we see Jane growing in confidence, learning the lesson of the brave front. The most comic incident in the book, it is also the most closely observed, and the most successfully executed. To see reluctant youngsters reading it, or even better to read it aloud to them, is one of those 'moments' when real absorption happens.

There are other ways too in which the book betters the run-of-the-mill magazine story. Jane may be the modern Cinderella figure – ordinary, nervous, self-effacing; with Marcy as the combined ugly sisters – and Stan may be her Prince Charming. But neither of them has anything anachronistic or sentimentally idealised. Jane is not a junior mistress in a boarding school, nor looking for a part in a film, singing in a Pop-group, or an up-and-coming private secretary living in a flat. Stan is not heir to a princely fortune, nor a successful young writer, a publicity agent, or an actor or Pop star. (He is, in fact, of all banal occupations, a dog's meat delivery boy.) The setting is not London or New York but Woodmont, which is American mid-country, small town. The parents are neither bad-tempered and weak disciplined (as in many modern English stories for older children) nor all sweetness and light and social sensitivity (as in so many American stories). There is no attempt to play up to motor-bikes, jazzy cars, or zippy clothes – the error of the newest attempts to write 'for' this market in this country (books like Marjorie Gayler's *Where There's a Wheel* and *Daphne Sets a Fashion*). Beverly Cleary has, in fact, a genuine sympathy and knowledge of unexciting ordinary teenagers, neither panders to them, nor exploits their most obvious forms of expression though she does seem wary of criticising them, except in her two-dimensional pseudo-villain creations, like the vamp Marcy, when she can expect a sympathetic agreement from her readers anyway. She is not moralistic in her attitude (as Penny Weston is in *Trend*'s story 'The Day I Left the Scene') nor so completely given only to the plot line that her writing is as anaemic and thread-bare as Blyton Neurosis literature. She has a genuine power of observation and an ability to catch it in a language that goes just deep enough to satisfy reluctant youngsters yet remain true and accurate, even if light-weight.

All this I find quite admirable, and it makes of *Fifteen* a touch-stone by which to judge literature of this type. That it stands alone is easy to discover; no other book, British or American, comes near it at the level of good entertaining fiction of a sufficiently truthful nature, and sufficiently skilful execution to wean reluctant readers among the girls on to better material than the magazines. It strides the rift and we could do with more, not like it but of the same stature and calibre, exploring as successfully the field of ordinary, common-or-garden, young people's lives.

Young Mother by JOSEPHINE KAMM, published by Brockhampton Press and Heinemann Educational Books' New Windmill Series.

Mrs. Kamm's book caused quite a storm in a tea-cup when it first appeared in 1965, and there are still public librarians who bar it from their shelves, as well as teachers who believe it to be a book young people should not read. Usually people take such a strong position because of the subject of the book. There are others who are highly critical of the book's literary merits: its style, the character on which the book places the moral responsibility for what happens, and such like.

Young Mother, as the title suggests, is concerned with illegitimacy. Pat Henley has a baby fathered by a vaguely described older man she meets at a friend's party. She is sent by her family (her father and mother are divorced, and there is an elder sister about to marry, and a younger teenage brother) to a Mrs. Wilkinson, away from town; then to a mother-and-baby home where the baby is born. Pat is persuaded to have her little boy, John, adopted, only to rebel for a time, during which she runs away to Mrs. Wilkinson who tries to let her make a go of keeping the child. Pat can't cope and at last allows the Bartletts to adopt, herself returning home. The book ends on Pat's sister's wedding day, and a note from Mrs. Bartlett hoping that one day Pat will marry and have children as wonderful as John.

I'm quite sure that its subject is what makes this book so very popular, as it is among girls. Mrs. Kamm has written much more skilfully – her *Out of Step*, a story about a white girl and her coloured boy-friend, for example – and I personally find *Young Mother* lacking in imaginative energy. I feel she has done a good deal of research into the problem and the results of that research have been worked into the plot, without it being sufficiently well absorbed in Mrs. Kamm's imagination first. There is a self-conscious heaviness about the style which gives the narrative the tone of a fictionalised casebook, rather than a story. One is led rather to view the ins and outs of having an illegitimate baby than to experience the situation through the character of Pat who is somehow never quite brought to life: she is very much the puppet of the narrative line.

I'm less disturbed than others by the apportioning of the blame. You can't apportion blame in such situations. Who is ever really 'to blame' when a girl has a baby like this? Yet one must recognise personal responsibility. One must say that Pat, like every girl in her place, must realise that she did have a say in the matter, and that only she can finally decide the yea's and nay's of the affair. Mrs. Kamm makes quite clear the *legal* right of the girl, the social difficulties, and the normal process by which the problem is handled. She does not, to my mind, realise well enough in the book the horror of the time. Not the moral horror – Lord forbid we should have in any book puritanical dwelling on the Hellish Evil of Sex – but the sad, wearying, conscience-stricken, brooding days of the time; the hatefulness of even the most well-run mother-and-baby home; the sensation of days which might, in the circumstances of a marriage and a young husband, have been happy, looked-forward-to and full of all the good things mothers tell us are so. This is the real heart of the matter which I look for in this book, and don't find.

Nor, I think, is the lack of it due in any way to any failure of Mrs. Kamm to see it, nor in any lack of potential in her as a story-teller, as a writer who could achieve such a realisation. I'm sure that she was so inhibited by the knowledge that she was treating a subject likely to cause dispute that, in her attempts to keep the story to acceptable limits, she avoided the very heart of the matter, so marring her book. Had she given the story the full treatment of truth – not case-book, legal truth, but the imaginatively presented living truth – there would have been a much bigger outcry than there was; and the book might in fact have become commercially unpublishable. Children's and young people's books in this country depend for their sales almost entirely on librarians and teachers. Incur their disfavour and you might as well give up as a writer and publisher. Their views tend to be conservative (publicly if not privately), they have a strong sense of duty to their charges and to 'literature'. Any book which seems to have morally dangerous qualities *and* literary faults will almost certainly receive a good deal of neglect – to put it all mildly. Mrs. Kamm must have understood this; and it affected her work on this book. She hoped to avoid 'trouble' by sticking closely to the case histories she researched so that the charge of unreality could easily be deflected. Her style reflects a desire to avoid any sensation of squalor, or harshness. It is polite, formal, restrained. The story itself avoids the 'delicate' moments. Thus the 'man' is a vague figure at a party, unseen again (evasion in the book even if too often a truth in reality), and the seduction scene is merely reported by Pat to her sister, not told as direct narrative. The birth scene is undescribed. The girls at the mother-and-baby home are remarkably 'level', both emotionally and in characteristics, for one of the places in the world where all sorts of the pleasant and not so pleasant are thrown together, and in very strained circumstances. As many people have pointed out, Pat's mother comes in for a lot of the bricks, and appears the blackened character as a result of the restraint exercised everywhere else. In fact, she is no less than an unsympathetic character.

Yet, despite all this, *Young Mother* is the only book for young people published in Britain which attempts to deal with anything as difficult by way of subject. That Mrs. Kamm's courage has been rewarded, that her instincts in writing the book were correct, are easy to see: the book is the most popular of any, and shares top place in the parade with *Fifteen*. It is read avidly and with obvious involvement by most girls and some boys. It is the subject that achieves this, for there is a thirst, a literary thirst, among young people whether reluctant or not, for books which deal imaginatively with the topics that occupy their thoughts, their worries, their daily lives. I would stress 'which handle imaginatively'. The 'non-fiction' books available, and the amount of teaching done on just such topics are great nowadays and growing still. But this is not enough. It is not enough in theory and one knows it is not enough in reality. One only has to observe how the creative fiction books which deal with such things are used to know this. You can give factual training as much as you like. Until it has been absorbed by the imagination – in other words it has been vitally experienced, either through living it directly, or through a well-handled imaginative treatment – then it is a *meaningless* collection of facts. This one argument, leave aside all the others, justifies to me the central place I would claim for the value of creative fiction reading.

In my own work among young people caught in the very situation dealt with in *Young Mother* I have heard the same words repeated: 'I didn't know what it all meant. I didn't know it was like this.' Not even after two years of direct teaching about 'it' and related topics during secondary school age. We shall come to the list of 'it's' soon, as we shall to a consideration of truth in books for the young. Here I merely want to emphasise the primacy of the subject in this book's success, and add to this that it is, like *Fifteen*, told very directly with few plot or character complications.

So far we seem to have discussed books read mainly by girls, and though this happened because they followed naturally from the discussion of their magazines, it is also true that it is not so easy to find any one or two quality books which succeed so completely among boys, whose reading is more diverse. In their reading, girls are a much more homogeneous group than the other sex. Nevertheless, there are some titles which have a very big following and which also demonstrate facets of the willingly engaged reading of reluctant boys.

The Day of the Triffids by JOHN WYNDHAM, published by Michael Joseph and Penguin.

John Wyndham has a strong following among both boys and girls over the age of 14. He is read remarkably far down the intelligence quotient of slow readers, and enjoyed as much by intelligent reluctant readers. *Triffids* is a long and by no means easy book (272 closely printed pages in the Penguin edition) and much the most popular of his books. I am constantly surprised by the variety of young people who discover him as an exciting, absorbing writer through this book.

What is at once striking about Wyndham, in *Triffids* particularly, is his natural, professional ability to tell a story, to make the most ordinary incidents exciting, to add on incident upon incident in a way that grips his reader. *Triffids*, beginning in the first startling moments of the strange events

by which 'The End Begins', full of action, uses Wyndham's gift of juxta-
posing the ordinary and the unusual so that each counterpoints the other:
Here is the opening paragraph:

> When a day that you happen to know is Wednesday starts off by sounding
> like Sunday, there is something seriously wrong somewhere.

You could not ask for a more direct and immediately engaging start. This
is no paste-and-scissors educational writer. This is the professional story-teller
at work. In a book so long, with such complex movements and ideas in it as
Triffids has for those who would find them, we begin with a short, snappy,
uncomplicated sentence that catches our interest by its suggestion of confusion
in the mixing of such mundane things as days of the week. Why is it that this
particular Wednesday is like a Sunday? Especially when one thinks of an
English Wednesday in the bustle of the week as against the deadness of an
English Sunday, with its empty spaces and echoing yawning streets. There
follows a detailed description of the movements of a man as he explores a
known world suddenly changed, in order to solve this strange mystery.
Naturally we are gripped; so gripped that Wyndham confidently spends the
twenty-six pages of Chapter Two (nine pages longer than the first chapter)
in a quite academic study of the arrival of the Triffids without anxiety about
the loss of readers. The Triffids themselves are a fascinating invention: one
wants to know as much as one can about them, and I well remember from
my own first reading of the book the desire for still more information when
that encyclopaedic second chapter closed. Similarly affected are most of his
'reluctant' young readers, and those who are glad to get through it are moved
to skip more by a desire to see the Triffids in action than through boredom
with Chapter Two.

The book has been criticised by at least one examination board to my
knowledge as a book unsuitable for examination purposes because it lacks
depth of characterisation. This strikes me as being a very short-sighted and
somewhat depressing comment. It is true that *Triffids* is not a book one
would use as an example of brilliantly explored characters; it is not intended
to be this. But it is also true that here we see the good story-teller at work;
that *Triffids* deals most entertainingly with all sorts of moral, philosophical,
political, social questions it would benefit any school pupil to discuss. It also
happens to have some of the most convincing and accurately imagined
descriptions of London and rural England in slow decline from neglect one
could hope to meet. They have a strangely eerie and moving effect on the

story and its atmosphere of truth. By these descriptions Wyndham manipulates our sense of time, of our own importance, and upsets our sense of
the permanence of things so that we are made to think *and to feel* (and this is
the important element to the reluctant reader) our littleness, our transitory
nature. And this is a theme which crops up in the thinking of young people:
they are concerned with their growing awareness of the size of the universe,
the nature of time, of their place in the scheme of things. And these things
concern them whether they have an I.Q. of 140 + or of 75, and though those
at the upper limit of that scale will explore the ideas more academically and
profoundly, it is just as important that those at the average and lower end of
the scale should have opportunity to do so too, by means which absorb and
involve them. They can, via *The Day of the Triffids*, entertainingly and
through writing of a not unskilful quality. Here is Wyndham tinkering
with our sense of time and permanence:

> And so I came to Westminster . . .
> Above it all rose the Houses of Parliament, with the hands of the clock stopped at
> three minutes past six. It was difficult to believe that all that meant nothing any more,
> that now it was just a pretentious confection in uncertain stone which could decay
> in peace. Let it shower its crumbling pinnacles on to the terrace as it would – there
> would be no more indignant members complaining of the risk to their valuable lives.
> Into those halls which had in their day set world echoes to good intentions and
> sad expediencies, the roofs could in due course fall; there would be none to stop
> them, and none to care. Alongside, the Thames flowed imperturbably on. So it would
> flow until the day the Embankments crumbled and the water spread out and
> Westminster became once more an island in a marsh. (p. 152.)

Three paragraphs later, Wyndham introduces another basic theme in
young people's thinking – indeed, young people, old people, small children:
it is a universal theme – loneliness:

> Moreover, I was beginning to experience something new – the fear of being alone.
> I had not been alone since I walked from the hospital along Piccadilly, and then
> there had been bewildering novelty in all I saw. Now, for the first time I began to
> feel the horror that real loneliness holds for a species that is by nature gregarious. I
> felt naked, exposed to all the fears that prowled. . . . (*Ibid.*)

(Note, in passing, the difficulty of Wyndham's vocabulary, which makes
his books just too difficult for readers who find many long, 'difficult' words
a real barrier, his vocabulary count being just too high to allow even an
increased reading rate to lift us clear of the verbal hedges.)

These are the elements which make Wyndham one of the most popular
'science fiction' authors of all: his world is usually our world, yet in this world

the strangest, and in Wyndham's hands, terrifyingly likely things happen. He handles the 'puzzles' like time, identity, personality; he has a knack of inventing just the right 'monster' – like the Triffids themselves, the best of all his inventions – and of creating them from a use of common-sense ideas and facts which lend them greater verisimilitude than most SF creations. His stories are seated in our lives now; his strange creations always described so much like a newspaper report and carefully documented that they never seem far-fetched. These things and a mature, adult approach – no kid's stuff here – make of Wyndham a popular author with people who would normally prefer not to bother with a book.

The pattern is emerging clearly: ability as a story-teller; themes of immediate concern to the young; a directness of approach more concerned with the actions of the story than with the finer points of character-delving; a sensation of the 'real now' handled in such a way that it is thrown into relief; a mature concern for what at this age are thought of as the important things in life – love, identity, courage and so on.

It is suchlike qualities which make of another quite different book a favourite with reluctant readers from the ages of 8 to 16:

The Boy Who Was Afraid by ARMSTRONG SPERRY, published by Bodley Head, Knight Books, and Heinemann Educational Books' New Windmill Series.

This very simply told, direct, unencumbered story is intended for the 8 to 12 year olds, but because it handles a sympathetic theme (cowardice turned to courage), and is finely told through action (there are no 'pondering passages' in all its 92 pages of the hardback version) it enjoys a readership far greater than originally intended. It seems to me to be one of the few prize-winning children's books that reluctants like! It was a Newbery Award winner.

The story of a Polynesian chief's son who is afraid of the sea, and goes out across the ocean accompanied only by his dog and a spirit-like albatross with a game leg, is caught in a storm and thrown eventually on to a volcanic island set apart as a taboo sacrificial place by 'the eaters of men', this book has about it all the favourite elements of children's books, yet still catches the teenager's interest, if he has not already read it. Naturally: because it deals with fear; because there are in the book constant physical conflicts: between the boy and the seas, the sacrificial idol-fear, the wild boar he kills, the shark he fights, the octopus which nearly puts an end to him, and at last the eaters of men themselves from whom he narrowly escapes. Linking these moments is the boy's concern with everyday needs: food, shelter, his project of building a canoe to carry him back home, and his natural, open, unembarrassed pleasure in proving his courage to his father and his contemporaries.

The Boy Who Was Afraid is widely recognised as being a quality book: the story, the writing, the moral and emotional framework please everyone, even if some are patronising about the obvious way it is all done. Let us remember that we are not all subtle diviners of the allegorically clothed fantasy, the story with deep and carefully hidden meaning. What Sperry does, he does with a sureness of touch, and a quality of imagination that makes his slim book a great story.

Here he is, bringing his coward–hero Mafatu up against his first dilemma. Mafatu couldn't avoid the storm, he had no option but to see it through. Now, with the sacred taboo idol suddenly before him, surrounded by the bones of human victims, shrouded in tribal legend about the dangers of incurring the wrath of the gods, the boy must make his own first act of courage, or slink away, defeated once more. Such a theme makes even more sense at 15 than it does at 8:

> He saw a series of wide stone terraces rising in a pyramid many feet high; on top of this pyramid a grotesque idol, hideously ugly, reared in the brilliant sunshine. It was an ancient idol, its contours softened with fungus and lichens, corroded by the rains of ages. The roots of convolvulus writhed about its base. No wind reached this hidden circle, and insects hummed in the hot air. Mafatu felt that he was stifling. His heart pounded. A *marae* – a Sacred Place. . . .
>
> . . . It was evident that the savages had been here recently, for the piles of ashes rested undisturbed by wind and storm. The cleared circle seemed to hold its breath, locked in a supernatural silence. As the boy paused, irresolute, looking up at the towering marae, his eye was caught and held by a gleam of light and his heart gave a mighty leap. For he saw that a spearhead lay on the sacred platform. Finely ground, sharp-edged; a spear for food, a weapon against attack. Dare he take it? It might mean death. . . . His heart pounded. He moved one foot forward. His hands were damp and cold. The flashing spearhead winked back at him like an evil eye. The boy's limbs turned to water. For a second he was powerless to move. In that moment had a score of black men leaped forth from the jungle he could not have stirred or cried. He fought for control. . . . Almost it seemed as if he could see dark shadows moving among the ferns and hear the phantom whisper of voices. But he edged forward, poised for instant flight. There – he was so close to the idol that he could have touched it. He reached out his hand. It took every ounce of will. The spearhead glistened brightly. . . . His fingers closed about it, tightened. The towering idol cast a shadow of darkness across the green earth. Quickly the boy drew the spearhead toward him. But in moving it he dislodged a bone. It fell at his feet. Its touch was deathly cold. Mafatu gasped. Then he whipped about and was running, But he still gripped the spearhead in his fist. (pp. 42, 44–46.)

Such directly described, well-imagined incidents as this attract reluctant readers. If we feel it is naive to a degree sophisticated boys and girls of 15 would find unacceptable, look at what may be a strange yet also perhaps apposite comparison, also read by many of these same boys and girls: James Bond. Take, for example, *Dr. No.* It bears unexpected likenesses to *The Boy Who Was Afraid*: Bond is out after a cause of fear (Dr. No terrifies the locals), crosses a sea, fights a dragon, meets an eater of men (No himself) and takes on a variety of dangerous obstacles, tangling finally, as does Mafatu, with a horror of the deep (in Bond's case a giant squid). If one wanted to be pseudo-psychological, one might suggest that Mafatu's faithful dog Uri, for whom Mafatu fights the shark, is paralleled by Honeychile, for whom Bond takes on the tortuous battles, running No's horror gauntlet through the tunnel. Mafatu's chieftain father is in the background for whom the entire expedition is begun; there is father-figure M behind Bond. Each book is set on an island different from the hero's home island. There is the villainous 'other tribe': the Black (as opposed to the brown) eaters of men for Mafatu; the yellow–black Chinese negroes for Bond. Courage, devotion to 'duty' or the M-figure, desire to prove one's self to one's self, physical conflict, the linking thread of 'everyday' living seen in relief against the unusual, exciting action – they are all there in both books. And the narrative is handled in a direct, unencumbered fashion. Read pages 139–41 of *Dr. No* as a comparison with the passage quoted from *The Boy Who Was Afraid*.

(It is interesting, as a side-issue, to look at the moment of death in a Fleming book. After all the pronouncements against him as an author for adults, never mind young people, about his violence and sadism, it remains true that he is much less given to graphic details of the horror of death, torture, love-making or pain than many a writer more highly thought of and quite happily given to children with much encouragement to read [like Forester, and Monsarrat, for example]. Compare the death of Quarrel and a page or two later when Bond pays his last respects to the body, with what Holbrook says about his touchstone in children's reading, *Huckleberry Finn* [*English for Maturity*, pp. 176 ff.]. Holbrook quotes a passage from *Finn*, describing the finding of Huck's dead father, and praises the economy of detail about the body, and the shift of focus at once to other things. Fleming does just this. Readers might be interested in a further study on these lines in Ann S. Boyd's *The Devil with James Bond*, published by Fontana and, even better, *The James Bond Dossier* by Kingsley Amis, published by Pan Books.)

On the basis of all this it is not surprising that these two authors are successful with reluctant readers; that both show clearly the basic elements necessary in reading for this age and person. Even if we disagree about Bond, we are unlikely to do so about *The Boy Who Was Afraid*. It is writing of quality, and is one of the books which demonstrate that reading material of value and quality can be as successful, and in my experience more successful than material of inferior quality. Adolescents reading Sperry for the first time will come back asking for more of him *before* asking for more of their usual Pop author. The sadness is that one has to say there is no more quite as good, quite as well-tuned to their tastes and needs.

That books which reluctant readers find attractive do not of necessity have to be of poor quality was substantiated whenever I put the question to a practitioner, as I did a number of times when preparing this book. Let me link together the two ideas which have run through this chapter and the preceding one: that reluctant readers read a good deal; and that the literature which appeals to them need not be of poor quality, and is often of high quality.

Two teachers first, as typical of the replies I received. The one from a grammar school in Bristol and the other a secondary modern in Castleford, Yorkshire.

The teacher-librarian, of the Bristol school was extraordinarily helpful, and conducted for me a complete survey of the 'stream' in the school which made least use of his library. Although, on average, boys in this stream were reading a book a fortnight, a hard core of reluctant readers read no fiction at all. The striking things about the survey were the normality of the sample and the teacher's pessimism at the existence of an unteachable minority, whose attitude was summed up in one answer: 'parents and teachers don't really understand my taste in reading, I have never found their help valuable'. A good deal of the books his reluctants read they find for themselves out of school. Yet his list of 'five star books' abstracted from the titles quoted by the boys reads as follows:

*H. G. Wells: half the sample mentioned *The War of the Worlds*.
Hammond Innes: half mentioned *Campbell's Kingdom*.
*John Buchan: a third mentioned *The Thirty-nine Steps*.
*Conan Doyle: nearly all mentioned Sherlock Holmes *short* stories.
John Wyndham: nearly all *The Day of the Triffids*, in strong preference to his others.

C. S. Forester: no one book mentioned more than another.

*Jerome K. Jerome: all mentioned *Three Men in a Boat* only.

Nevil Shute: *On the Beach.*

*Jules Verne: *20,000 Leagues Under the Sea.*

Ronald Welch: all the Carey Books.

Of these the most popular were:

* War of the Worlds
* The Thirty-nine Steps
  Campbell's Kingdom
  The Day of the Triffids

To these must be added the prevalence of W. E. Johns among his first year boys, and *Jack Schaefer's *Shane* among the third years. As well as Fleming's Bond, Charteris, Arthur C. Clarke, Maclean among the older forms.

Those books and authors distinguished by an asterisk are all given their bill of clearance by David Holbrook in *English for Maturity*, whose list is the most uncompromising one available in context of an argued position for their selection as 'good' reading. By any standard, however, this is acceptable reading.

The teacher, in commenting on my request for his opinion about reluctant readers inevitably accepting only poor quality literature, wrote:

> The reluctant reader will never get to grips with close character analysis or find themes and morals in what he reads. *Brave New World* they read at first purely as science fiction, and just don't relate it to this world. *Lord of the Flies* is liked purely for its horror, and *A Diamond as Big as the Ritz* purely for the luxuriant wealth it describes. No one mentioned [in the survey] the importance of human interest. Popular fiction need not be of poor quality, but it might as well be for all the reluctant reader sees in it, without the help of a teacher.

This comment begs a number of questions. Perhaps most of all it leads to a discussion of the effect of literature when the reader is unaware of its quality or its depth. And to this we must come. But the relevant note at this point is that near-aside: 'Popular fiction need not be of poor quality. . . .'

The same conclusion was reached by Mr. Tom Wild in Castleford. Tom Wild is an unorthodox teacher: his list of Five Star Books is the most unusual one could hope to meet: indeed it would be surprising to find quite the same books quoted in connection with reluctant readers by anyone else. It included *To Kill a Mocking Bird*, Durrell's *Bitter Lemons*, Remarque's *All Quiet on the Western Front* and books of a similar, I would have thought, forbidding nature, especially for secondary modern children of a less able kind. That Tom Wild manages to create a readership for them is the result of his own personality, taste and skill as a teacher. His comment on how much reluctants read and the inevitability of poor quality in books at a popular level was this:

> Yes. The reluctant reader does read a fair amount outside. Tho' I'm surprised at the few who willingly read the newspapers. Most of them are limited to *Roxy*, *Fab*, *Rave*, etc. Pernicious publications! The frightening thing about fringe reading is that it makes no demands on their vocabulary or comprehension. It is at best a palliative and I'm sure that a diet of this deadens the growing adolescent's desire to explore. The effort necessary for struggling with words is no longer there. . . .
>
> No, I do not think that there is any need for a book to be of poor quality for it to be popular. *Tom Sawyer* will readily disprove that. I do think, however, that the methods of marketing are infinitely better organised when it comes to shoddy goods. And even many adults regard reading as a soporific or erogenous activity all too often, and are inclined to choose rubbish for train journeys, bedside reading, etc.

Again something of the pessimism of tone (common to most of us who have to do with young people's reading – it is an occupational disease). But the same conclusion, along with a new vein of thought – that about marketing – to which we will return.

Yet one more comment: this time by Mrs. Sheila Ray, until recently Children's and Youth Librarian working in Leicestershire. Mrs. Ray, like most of the librarians responsible for the young people's library service, sees more than merely the 20 per cent who use the libraries. She had to deal with every type of school and youth centre, supplying their requests, and in Mrs. Ray's case at least, is particularly concerned about reluctant readers and making special efforts to reach them directly through her work. I asked her what her Five Star Books were. She was very certain:

> *A Kind of Loving*, *Young Mother*, *The Day of the Triffids* (or most of Wyndham), *A Town Like Alice* (or nearly any of Shute's), and Beverly Cleary's *Fifteen*.

When I asked what she would say to the idea that books do not have to be of inferior quality before the submerged 60 per cent will read them, she answered: 'I'm sure this is true. I think the submerged sixty per cent will read the stuff we approve if it is put in their way – and in the right way. Or at least some of the sixty per cent will.'

Finally, a bookseller, Mr. A. H. Howells of Parry Books Ltd., Liverpool. I contacted him and other booksellers who know this market. I quote his remarks, not only because they are typical, but because Mr. Howells has studied the reluctant adolescent, has very close links with all sorts of schools in which he runs book agencies, and therefore knows from direct experience on what the young spend their money in all sorts of educational establishments.

> The following subjects appear to be most popular: GHOST STORIES: Poe, Halifaxe, etc. ANIMAL STORIES: Durrell, *Born Free, Ring of Bright Water*. SCIENCE FICTION: Wyndham, Clarke, Lewis, H. G. Wells. (I am continually amazed at the demand for say *War of the Worlds*, and also for Sherlock Holmes.) Also *Fifteen, Lord of the Flies, 1984, Brave New World, Saturday Night and Sunday Morning, Three Men in a Boat, 1066 and All That.* FILM TIE-UPS: *Sound of Music, Mary Poppins, Dr. Zhivago.* WAR STORIES: *Wooden Horse, Reach for the Sky, The Small Woman, Dawn of D Day, The Longest Day.*

In an earlier letter Mr. Howells said 'I am sure that the biggest untapped market in publishing lies in this field'. I would agree with that very firmly stated opinion, and all it implies about the present situation and what could be.

It is quite surprising when one considers the possible range of books that could be mentioned, that the same ones, my Five Star Books, crop up time and again.

For my purposes at present I must take certain things as now established:

1. Reluctant readers do in fact read a good deal more material than we often imagine is so.
2. The quality of that material ranges from rock bottom to a very acceptable quality, if not the classic best.
3. There are certain titles everyone seems to find useful, titles of acceptable quality, 'Five Star Books', and these are listed in Appendix A.
4. There seem to be various themes and technical factors which affect the success of the book, and these it would be profitable to explore more deeply.
5. There seems to be no reason why the material read and produced for this age should not be of good quality if it is to be popular and commercially viable: it is not true that it will inevitably be of poor quality if they are willing to read it.
6. A good deal of the material we provide in 'children's lists', fondly imagining it right for 'them', is far off target. We must look closely at our standards and ideas about children's books generally (reluctance doesn't just happen at 13 or some such arbitrary age, but has its seeds in earlier years) and at young people's fiction in particular.

7. There are already suggesting themselves factors other than the material itself, which help or hinder the growth of a valid reading habit among the submerged 60 per cent.

We must now, it seems, tackle firmly and head-on a two-headed problem: relevance of the books produced, and our pre-conceptions about what is right, allowable, and valuable in young people's reading.

4

It's Good For You

I MAKE no apology for quoting Bettina Hürlimann to my own ends. In her book *Three Centuries of Children's Books in Europe*, she ends her Introductory history like this:

> For in this restless age of technology, when the emphasis is always on records of attainment and higher productivity, there is some danger of forgetting that a child does not require too much in the way of books. What he does need are the right books at the right time so that he may find in literature a true point of balance in an often disordered life. It is for us as parents or teachers, librarians or publishers, to recognise this need and to know how best, how most imaginatively, to fulfil it. (p. xviii.)

If only we could learn that lesson, drill that point of view into our heads so that when we come to judge, select, present books 'right' for 'children' (of all ages) we might get nearer the mark than we so often do at present.

Since 1945, the great watershed in children's book production, 'things', we are told, 'have happened'. Words like 'revolution', 'crises', 'flowering', 'explosion' are used, often meaninglessly, often hysterically, often with un-critical regard for what has actually happened. True, the children's book market has become a commercially valuable one, and that expansion still goes on – is almost in fact worthy of 'boom' talk. Certainly, children's book production has 'developed', though I reserve my comments on that develop-ment. Certainly, writers for children are regarded with greater seriousness than they were. Instead of being 'rewards', they are valued at about a third of the financial outlay credited to their 'adult' author colleagues. That is improvement – I suppose.

But I often feel that the enthusiasm one encounters for the present state and trends in children's books has about it a lack of perception of the real lines of development that is almost dangerously myopic.

In 1936 the first Carnegie Medal was presented to an undoubted master-craftsman, Arthur Ransome. Since then it has gone to equally fine spirits:

Walter de la Mare, Eleanor Farjeon, and C. S. Lewis. As the accolade of success and achievement it surely presents a selective view of what we believe to be worthwhile in books for children. These books should reflect our standards of quality, our judgement of what is 'right' for children, and the Medal itself our means of recognition of a writer, and an encouragement to others to work to such standards. The Library Association's *Chosen for Children*, an account of the writers awarded the Medal between 1936 and 1957, states:

> Critics have sometimes faulted the assessors for awarding the Medal to a writer whose appeal is to a rather limited audience. This is to apply the democratic principle blindly. The Medal is not awarded as the result of a plebiscite; it is awarded by a small body of experts who bring to the assessment of the eligible books high standards of criticism and long experience of books and their readers. These judges are unlikely to be attracted by facile or meretricious qualities. This is not to say that the Carnegie Medal books are unpopular with children. A book for children, however excellent in style, integrity and accuracy, is a failure if it lacks the elusive quality of personality which makes it acceptable to its audience. . . . A test of the good children's book, as of a book for adults, is that it receives the commendation of discriminating readers. (p. 2.)

In 1966 no award was made. The 1965 choice was Philip Turner's *The Grange at High Force*, a book very typical of the O.U.P. productions which have figured often of late in the list. Let us examine what standards 'discriminating readers' commend. Bear in mind throughout the discussion that we are attempting to understand the nature of reluctance, and to find causes of it and some keys to its remedy.

Approach *Grange* as a child will approach it:

Demy 8vo, 220 pages, heavy paper. A bigger book in height and thickness than most on the shelves. To a reluctant reader this is itself forbidding.

Jacket shows a Papas coloured cartoon-style figure, back-view, carrying a shepherd's crook, and wearing snow-shoes. There is little here of immediate appeal: it is very sophisticated 'bookish' design and execution.

We try the blurb, the next most important consideration for the majority of children.

> Arthur Ramsgill was in a precarious position. He was standing in a niche in All Saints' Church, Darnley Mills, conducting 'Operation Bird's Nest'. Below him he could see the anxious faces of his friends Peter Beckford and David Hughes. Above him wisps of straw protruded from the pigeon's nest that he was trying to dislodge from its position in a window over the Lady Chapel altar. . . .
>
> 'Operation Bird's Nest' was to lead the three boys to investigate the mystery of the long-lost statue that once stood in the niche. . . .

It is unlikely that our submerged 60 per cent are still reading: the book is more likely to be back on the shelf. However, let's give the book the benefit of the doubt. Let's look at the opening:

> Arthur Ramsgill took one hand off the ladder and ran it through the stiff brush of his flaxen hair. At this height in Darnley Church it seemed much hotter than it did in his normal position in the sanctuary. A voice called up to him from below. 'Now don't be for starting physical jerks, he says. 'Tisn't a gym-a-nasium, and Old Charlie don't want for to have to clean your gore off of the tilery.' It was the voice of Charlie Bastable the All Saints' verger, one of the best known characters of the mill and market town of Darnley Mills, which was perched step below step down the steep staircase of the valley-side from the high moors to the curve of the river.

Compare this with the opening of *Fifteen*, or *The Day of the Triffids*, indeed with most of the Five Star Books listed, and one may readily see why *Grange at High Force* could not be described as an appealing book on its own merits. With promotion from a sympathetic librarian or teacher, it will be read by those whose stamina is muscular. Most children will leave the book alone otherwise. (Nor, merely to make a personal point, do I very much blame them. I find Turner's style self-conscious, his situations cerebrally contrived, and his story lacking in the first element of any good story: the quality of compulsion – he does not stir my curiosity and hold it. He has yet to learn what Miss Blyton, Capt. Johns, and those often derided popular authors have as their main talent: the market-place tale-teller's ability to hold our attention.)

The Grange at High Force is typical of the kind of book, in story, writing, and production, which, over the last ten years, has come to be considered, it seems, by 'discriminating readers' *among adults*, the epitome of good-quality children's literature. It is intellectual, sophisticated, over-written, unremarkable for anything in the slightest 'questionable' in thought, word or deed. It reflects an adult's rather sentimental view of childhood. It is passionless, cautious in its opinion, conservative in its theme and treatment. It is one of 'the well-produced books of good quality' that gives a glow of satisfaction when, dressed in their sparkling plastic covers, they line the library shelves, and the publisher's offices. There in the main they stay. In a way one is grateful they do. Yet what a waste of time and effort; and what an encouragement to reluctance!

In the same year as Turner's book received the Medal, the runner-up was *Elidor* by Alan Garner. And this again points up the nature of the accolade. It would have been a scandal if *Elidor* had been overlooked altogether. It is a disgrace that it was not given preference to Turner. Garner is a genuine artist, a writer of real and, I believe, massive talent. When *Elidor* was commended and Turner awarded the Medal, Garner had published *Weirdstone of Brising-amen*, and its sequel *Moon of Gomrath*. Both books surpass anything Turner had done (only *Colonel Sheperton's Clock* before *The Grange*). As a piece of writing *Elidor* has more truthful vitality in its first chapter than Turner achieves throughout his 220 word-packed, demy 8vo pages. If one wants to go further, its illustrator was, among 'discriminating readers', an even more popular and certainly more acceptable one than Papas: Charles Keeping. *Elidor*, by its power and the skill of its writing, even though a more complex idea than Turner's, commands a far wider potential audience and is reached from the shelves far more often by that audience because of its jacket, blurb and format.

Its opening confirms that choice:

> 'All right', said Nicholas. 'You're fed up. So am I. But we're better off here than at home.'
> 'It wouldn't be as cold as this', said David.
> 'That's what you say. Remember how it was last time we moved? Newspapers on the floor, and everyone sitting on packing cases. No thanks!'
> 'We're spent up,' said David. 'There isn't even enough for a cup of tea. So what are we going to do?'
> 'I don't know. Think of something.'
> They sat on the bench behind the statue of Watt. The sculptor had given him a stern face, but the pigeons had made him look as though he was just very sick of Manchester.
> 'We could go and ride on the lifts in Lewis's again,' said Helen.
> 'I've had enough of that,' said Nicholas. 'And anyway, they were watching us: we'd be chucked off.'
> 'What about the escalators?'
> 'They're no fun in this crowd.'
> 'Then let's go home,' said David. 'Hey, Roland, have you finished driving that map?'

And the story is away. There is insight into children here at an adult level, stated in a fashion children themselves respond to immediately. The writing is direct, truthful, firmly based in the known – it is amusing, it is so exactly 'as things are' – and by the end of the book the child has been taken on a step, led to the unknown in no small sense. The last chapter of *Elidor* is one of the fine things in children's books since Lewis finished *Narnia*, though in no way a copy of him. Yes, the bind is less permanent, and the size less forbidding than *The Grange*. But what a judgement on the selectors that they should, in the light of such things, choose *The Grange* rather than *Elidor*!

This sort of thing has happened before. In 1963 John Rowe Townsend's

Hell's Edge was runner-up to Hestor Burton's *Time of Trial*. One could make the same remarks about these two books as about the 1965 pair, except that Townsend has not the same massive talent as Garner.

Children's books are bought mainly by librarians and teachers. The librarians award the Medal; many teachers are guided very much by such 'expert' judgements, for many teachers are woefully ill-informed about children's books generally and the latest ones in particular.

Nevertheless, it is often forgotten that the public librarians see only 40 per cent of the population at most: that 40 per cent who, we may optimistically guess, use the public libraries. Only the really active schools service librarians ever see the 60 per cent who never set foot in the public libraries. Therefore this 'expert' judgement is bound to be biased by the reactions of the bookish 'willing' readers among children and influenced by the bookish adult tastes of the librarians. Thus the standards at present prescribed are:

> great length;
> intellectual style and treatment;
> sophisticated presentation and illustration;
> solid composition;
> inoffensive themes and subjects, or at least uncommitted, cautious treatment of anything likely to be 'doubtful';
> care in pleasing adults rather than children, for these are the ones who buy and judge, award and recommend.

I am sure the Carnegie Committee will feel I am maligning their purpose; will have many arguments to discount all I say, yet one cannot but feel that all this is so, whether by design or accident I would not conjecture. The award, they will say rightly, can only be made to the best of what is there. Yet this in itself seems to me to epitomise the state of children's books at present. Many of the people who *could* influence the movement of books most strongly follow hand-to-mouth behind what is done. The reviewers review (often months after publication dates) on the basis of that one book, without reference to any wider vision. The librarians award their Medal only on the basis of what has come out without any thought, apparently, for the trends they ought to encourage (one would have thought my example of Turner–Garner relevant here: which author, which of the two books would one prefer to encourage? The Medal Committee suggest Turner. If they did so in the light of future development as a result of their encouragement then my faith in them as a Committee is shaken to the foundations. One can only

hope they chose the Turner without such thought being taken into account).
What is the thinking which guides such choice? It surely cannot be that
the strategy is worked out in relation to what is so? The facts are that only
about 40 per cent of the population use the libraries, and, so far as hard-cover
books are concerned, fewer still buy at all regularly. The percentage of private
individuals who buy children's hard-back fiction is negligible. True, there
are other factors involved in the creation of such a situation, but one of them
certainly is that we produce books no one cares to buy. Within such a situation it is suicide to present these same books year after year as the choicest
gifts that can fall from the Heavens. They are, in the end, books which satisfy
a certain bookish minority, and that a very professional bookish minority;
they have little relevance and no meaning for the vast majority of children
and adults (most of whom never see them, and of those who do most don't
want to see them again). Are the 'discriminating readers' only those who can
enjoy such books? Is this the standard by which we decide who is discriminating and who is not? Are these 'experts' concerned to do as Bettina
Hürlimann wisely suggests: provide 'the right books at the right time' and
do they 'recognise this need and . . . know how best, how most imaginatively
to fulfil it'? (See footnote at the end of this chapter.)

Other factors operate besides these in the creation of reluctance directly by
what we suggest should be read and provide as 'good' books.

A major one is the emphasis on historical fiction. Such stories occupy
inordinate space in publishers' lists, and receive far more space and discussion
in the journals, outside the 'non-fiction' columns, than any other kind of
story. It is only to be expected that writers of an inferior kind (there are more
of these than better ones) should flee to historical settings for their stories. By
doing so they are relieved of a number of problems difficult to solve in stories
with contemporary settings, known to the author by experience. Your
standpoint can be much more dispassionate; you can focus on the fascinating
details of everyday life in days gone by which are easier to handle attractively
than similar details in daily life of the now. You are allowed to include in
your story pretty well as much gore, violence, sin and strife as you have a
mind to use (worded, of course, in suitably historical phrases and terms). This
is not allowed in contemporary books for the young (though one *is* allowed
to feed the same youngsters adult books which deal far more openly than
any children's book is likely to do with far worse topics than any children's
book is likely to handle, all at a level too deep for the child to absorb healthily.
You can do this and get away with it. Or, of course, one can just give them

the daily paper and no one will worry at the sensational handling of sin they will encounter there.) You can get away with a much less accurate ear for dialogue than is allowed if you are employing contemporary characters in contemporary speech. You can be 'poetic'. You can point a moral more easily and without losing your reader who somehow expects history to teach him lessons. (Children's writers love pointing morals.) You have not all the bother of accuracy. (Much is made of the 'accuracy' of the best modern historical novels. But this is a researched accuracy, 'factual' truth, not the truth of behaviour and manner which, if one is writing about the now, is so well known for any slip to be at once apparent. In historical novels such truth cannot be so easily tested. We feel we do not know at first hand if things were as they are now and so there is an easy suspension of disbelief.)

Thus historical fiction is an attractive form for many writers. I cannot say that I have found reluctant readers very often attracted to it as literature they can accept willingly. Most successful is Henry Treece as published by Brockhampton. The writer most often praised in this field, Rosemary Sutcliff, is found much too bookish a writer to be successful with reluctant readers, apart from her *The Eagle of the Ninth*, which enjoys a mild popularity.

I have had it said to me by a publisher's editor that children do not like contemporary settings and realism in their story books, particularly settings in their own social environment. I find it hard to accept this: E. W. Hildick's books, Reginald Maddock's *The Pit* and *The Widgeon Gang*, Josephine Kamm's *Young Mother* and *Out of Step*, John Rowe Townsend's *Gumble's Yard*, Joan Tate's books, S. G. Watt's *Number 21*, all these are immensely popular among children just like the ones portrayed, far more popular than any historical novel I know of. Added to which, most of these books are far better written than most historical novels. Indeed it would be odd if children did not want to read about their own world: they are interested in their own world, it concerns them and, just as adults do, they will make popular any book which handles the contemporary world well. The point is that it is more difficult to handle the contemporary world well. One could hardly find any books more popular than *Saturday Night and Sunday Morning, A Kind of Loving, Alfie, Room at the Top* (and they are not popular only because of the films made from them) and all the other major successes of the past twenty years which purport to deal with contemporary society. It has always been so and at all ages. And still is. But it must be well done.

Emphasis on the 'Classic' is another factor directly leading to reluctance. Edward Blishen has pointed out (*Children's Book News* No. 7, 1966):

It's a matter of sad fact that we have reduced the term 'Classic' to the level of what a child I once knew would describe as an ugh-word. I believe that if we want these unfortunate great books really to be read by the young we have to avoid, of course, all cheap and nasty reprints: but we have to be wary, also, of series that coo over the notion that a book is a 'Classic'. The best series are austere and make as little fuss as possible about the classic stature of the text. And the very best editions appear, like those of Puffins, democratically and diplomatically unstressed – books that, because they look like others, leave it to the young themselves to discover that, indeed, they are really like no other books whatever!

It is in fact, the infernal interference by the adult which so often creates reluctance, by recommending books not tuned to the needs of the child at that time, by making sacred cows of certain writers and books, by the damnation of 'You must read this – it's good for you!' (Like the man with his weeping child walking along the beach. The child is crying and asking to go home. The man is clipping the child's ear and saying 'I've brought you here to enjoy yourself, and enjoy yourself you *will*!')

'The right books at the right time' and the opportunity to meet the books without any preconceived suggestions about what is good for us to read. These seem to be emerging as lines of approach for handling the reluctant reader and books. We must say much more about them soon. Before then, having tried to suggest that the standards we have erected are bookish, intellectual, strategically thoughtless standards (and, I would say, far from critically acceptable standards) we must look for a page or two at what we will allow into children's books. I am sure that yet another factor in the creation of reluctance is the irrelevance of a good deal of older children's literature to the life the child leads. In other words, to fall back on my opening quotation, older children do not find in their books 'a true point of balance in an often disordered life'. Naturally, therefore, they look elsewhere for that point of balance: to other activities, other forms of expression.

I have already suggested how much more advanced than books are the girls' magazines in their provision for such needs, in their awareness of the things that are important in adolescence, and their willingness to handle them unembarrassedly.

It is interesting to compile a list from one's own common-sense knowledge of young adolescents and their concerns, and to match it with a list of books which take up these things as themes, and deal with them without also wrapping them up in respectable envelopes: envelopes like the historical novel, fantasy, science fiction or some other concealment device. (Many of these things do not even get an airing in this way, either.)

Here is my list of some of the concerning things in early adolescence.

Sex. As between boys and girls and between members of the same sex. Marriage and early married life.

Sex, plain animal appetite, is something every child has thrust at him from the moment he opens his eyes and ears. Because of this, as well as the natural operation of biology, the adolescent is preoccupied with this topic. The handling of it in creative quality-literature is anaemic, to say the least. It is completely absent from the Medal literature. It is handled only at a 'romantic' suggestive level by most teenage magazine material. There are one or two attempts at it in books of a reasonable standard for the market. And it is always boy-girl stuff. There has never, to my knowledge, been any attempt to handle the topic in any direct, mature way. (*Sam and Me* by Joan Tate comes nearest to succeeding here.) Any attempt to write about adolescent homosexual themes directly would be quite out of the question in the present climate of older-children's books. There is, of course, a great deal of it just below the surface of many children's books of all qualities.

Marriage, of course, is a closed book in any literature intended for young people. One of the most important events in most lives is used as a convenient climax finish on the last page of those books which even mention the event. The young person has to go to adult books for any imaginative re-creation of the event and the early days of married life, and the best of these books are very mature complex works; books like D. H. Lawrence's *The Rainbow*, for example. This is, in fact, for young people's writers, an open field.

Parents. One of the central themes. Rebellion against parents is normal at this age. It is very much in evidence and takes almost ritual forms today. It is added to by the problem of the first generation grammar school child. These are young people who have often lost contact with their parents because of the barriers thrown up by their education. No one has done any direct creative work on it, though Townsend touches on it in *Hell's Edge* and *Hallersage Sound*, and Garner in *The Owl Service* to rather greater effect. Now that there are writers emerging who have been through this particular mill, one hopes some relevant and exciting teenage books might appear dealing with the theme.

Authority. This links of course with parents, but I mean the authority which is of a different nature because it is not concerned in the family. That is: employers, police and the law, the gang, and importantly, school teachers.

This is a more frequently encountered theme in conventional children's books, but again it is often sub-theme, nothing more than an undercurrent. It has never been handled creatively to the extent that it enters the real lives of young people.

It is not after all just a straight 'adolescent-against-adult-rule' theme. It bears upon the young person in his relationship with his contemporaries, who often claim a loyalty which the child has been taught is wrong, like hiding a wrong-doer, following an anti-adult trend (in haircuts, clothes and the like), breaking long-standing family rules to satisfy a girl- or boy-friend, or the gang.

Work. It is in adolescence that work becomes a present fact rather than a contemplated future. It causes more upset than we remember – or than most of us professional book people, with our school–college–profession career ever knew – and yet it is a theme dealt with in any depth only in adult litera- ture of which I'm critical as valid adolescent reading. Like sex, it is a topic being beaten to a dull death by in-school discussion lessons about school-to- work problems and practicalities. Of course, if a writer were even tastefully honest about what many of these young people will find at work, the books would be banned. That it is a theme which means more than most one knows from reactions to passages concerned with early days of work in some of Sid Chaplin's novels, Llewellyn's *How Green was My Valley*, D. H. Law- rence's *Sons and Lovers*, and the modern situations in the books of Sillitoe, Barstow and, on an easier level, Joan Tate. There is very little of it in books for older children.

This same heading might include money and the many stories it provides as a central theme. Adult literature uses it a lot; young people's literature rarely. Yet young people spend more in 'pocket-money' terms more freely than any other section of the population.

The self. Most literature deals with this, I agree. But adolescence is particu- larly concerned with itself. Particularly it dwells on the strong feelings: loneliness, passion, failure, success (and the possibilities of them), physical appearance, feelings of inadequacy, moodiness, loves and hates, one's place in society, and the physical universe. Opinions are strongly held, ideas are thrusting to the forefront of thought. So we could go on. It is all contained in any standard textbook on adolescence. But it seems to have evaded the powers of good writers to catch it in books for the people involved. Most of all the hot-and-cold extremes, and the sudden fluctuations between almost violent gaiety and violent depression have never been well handled in young people's novels, though again they have sometimes been in adult novels.

The standard problems. These open up a possible field for the story I'd have thought attractive to novelists. They include things like illegitimacy, criminal actions and life under punishment and cure, drugs, ill-health, death, shyness, war, the vote, drink, smoking, swearing, colour and race. It would be tedious to go on. Their name is Legion.

I've said nothing yet about the virtues that genuinely absorb young people: heroism, courage, physical endurance; nor about the wish-fulfilment topics: success, fame, and the struggle for these things. Naturally there is an equal interest in the opposites: cowardice, and great wickedness. And these things have their greatest effect when set in among such other topics as we have listed above. Thus there was a greater interest among teenagers in (to go to the film for aid) Kazan's *Rebel Without a Cause* than in Welles' *Citizen Kane*. Teenagers, I'm sure, more than any other age want to discuss living through other people of their own age doing things than through much older people doing things which involve the themes under discussion. (Bond is an interesting sidelight here. I would guess that most people reading Fleming see Bond as the age they most prefer him to be. There is much about him that is boyish – it's one of the things other characters, especially women, like about him. And this is what makes him successful with teenagers, who can think of him just exactly as they want. His age is in fact pretty indefinite. Early in the Saga, as Amis points out, he is said to be approaching 45, but the later books require a recalculation which puts Bond's age in the earliest stories at 15! By any standards, Bond's activities are those of a young man.)

These are some of the major themes that one would expect in books for young people. A matching list of available books is somewhat inadequate:

Young Mother by JOSEPHINE KAMM. Illegitimacy.
Out of Step by JOSEPHINE KAMM. Colour problem.
Fifteen by BEVERLY CLEARY. Dating.
The Pit by REGINALD MADDOCK. Social deprivation and prejudice; authority and loyalty.

The Joan Tate Books: very short stories which neatly deal with many such things in an uncomplicated way.

Sam and Me by JOAN TATE. Independence in a relationship of love. Inability to communicate.

Gumble's Yard and *Widdershins Crescent* by J. R. TOWNSEND. The family and social and cultural poverty.

Hell's Edge by J. R. TOWNSEND. A sub-plot of regional and class problems faced by a teenage boy and girl.

Walkabout by JAMES VANCE MARSHALL. Boy–girl awakening.

The Boy Who Was Afraid by ARMSTRONG SPERRY. Courage.

To Clear the River by JOHN BERRINGTON. Teenage relations and an attempt to handle the topics they talk about and which concern them (but a book sadly dull in plot).

As a May Morning by GRACE HOGARTH. Girl growing up.

Marianne and Mark by CATHERINE STORR. Girl becoming aware of boys and having difficulty adjusting the relationships.

The Boy from Hackston N.E. by REGINALD TAYLOR. Boy faced with a choice between decency and dishonesty, forced on him by his social circumstances.

Cycle Smash by AIDAN CHAMBERS. Boy faced with recovery after physical disablement.

Marle by AIDAN CHAMBERS. Boy faced with mundane life safely in a city or uncertain life doing something more worth while but challenging, and away from 'with-it' circles.

Beat of the City by H. F. BRINSMEAD. Teenage life in Sydney, Australia. (Needs reading stamina.)

The Owl Service by ALAN GARNER. Teenagers caught in a clash of backgrounds and parental influences.

These are some books of a good standard in their writing which go some way towards the provision of this basic, essential literature for the ages 11 to 16. (One might add the Pan-Macmillan Topliners, a paperback series deliberately setting out to supply these needs in good books.) Yet it is a small list compared with the lists one could compile of other books in other categories (historical, science fiction, etc.) It is a depressing list for this reason. John Rowe Townsend, in his outline of children's literature, *Written for Children* (Garnet Miller), sums it up like this:

Those of us who are concerned with books tend to assume that young people, if they read at all, will be reading adult novels before they are far into their teens. So they will; but I do not know what right we have to assume that adult books will meet all their needs, any more than adult recreations meet all their needs. Promoters of 'pop' culture have been quick to sense a teenage market; serious authors and publishers have too often averted their eyes. I think we have neglected an opportunity, maybe an obligation. There are matters such as starting work (or staying at school), striking out new relationships with parents and with the adult world, coming to terms with the opposite sex, and above all discovering what kind of person you really are, that are of the utmost interest to adolescents but that are not often dealt with in adult fiction, or at least not dealt with in ways that seem helpful. I have often heard it said that we should not emphasise the separateness of the teenager; nor should we; but we do not help him by going on as though he either didn't exist or was a deplorable and temporary phenomenon. I should like to see many more good, lively books about modern life which would not seem 'kids' stuff' to people in their early and middle teens. (pp. 145–6.)

The good and lively books about modern life, which Townsend, myself and a goodly number of other people would like to see, will not be written until we – parents, teachers, librarians and publishers – have resolved our minds about the question of how much can be told of truth in the language of reality to young people in books intended for them.

Unless we are honest about the situation into which we are trying to present better, more meaningful, more entertaining books for young people, then our work will be in vain. And if we are honest about the situation as at present concerning permissible language, subjects and treatments we can say something like this:

The accepted 'classics' and lighter books of earlier decades, historical novels nowadays and some fantasy often contain scenes, subjects and treatments which, if written in modern language in contemporary settings, would be disallowed and excluded from libraries. Thus *Oliver Twist* discusses and portrays the corrupt practice of a frightening character, Fagin, the murder of a prostitute by her adulterous lover and burglar pal with whom she has been living for years in conditions of the most sordid kind. Throughout the book there are scenes in which officialdom is duped, the law made laughable and the public services made to look pretty ineffectual. All this is acceptable because it concerns an historical time, and because the book is counted the achievement of a master of novel form – a truthful critique of a once (but now no longer?) real state of affairs.

The entertainment literature of the last century, and a good deal of similar 'middle literature' of this kind, contains some suspect material if one wants to be pernickety about such things. *Treasure Island* treats one of literature's most alive and immoral characters, Long John Silver, entirely sympathetically, and the original story has even been adapted (as it was in the Walt Disney film of the book) to allow Long John to escape back into the world unpunished and with a physiometric leer which, on a last curtain, can mean nothing less than that Silver intends to pursue his wicked works elsewhere. Jim Hawkins is not the last young teenager who will be clawed and misused by the one-legged pirate. The interesting thing is that Disney presumably made the alteration just because we have grown to love Long John so much that a tragic, punitive ending was sentimentally too upsetting for popular taste. No one has ever condemned either Stevenson for his original creation nor Disney for what he did to Stevenson's character (apart from the academic criticism that such alteration is a regrettable tampering with an author's work – and even this criticism reached no very great proportions). Instead we all saw the film and cooed about it. Certainly, no one finds *Treasure Island* 'dangerous' material to feed to children.

In our desperation to find books that will satisfy the needs of teenage reluctant readers there is now a strong advocacy for the use of 'suitable' contemporary adult novels. Among the titles usually suggested as successful are these:

Saturday Night and Sunday Morning by ALAN SILLITOE.
A Kind of Loving by STAN BARSTOW.
Absolute Beginners by COLIN MACINNES.
The Wind is Green by JANE WHITE.
The Cruel Sea by NICHOLAS MONSARRAT.
Room at the Top by JOHN BRAINE.
Catcher in the Rye by J. D. SALINGER.
Brighton Rock by GRAHAM GREENE.
Lucky Jim by KINGSLEY AMIS.
The Prime of Miss Jean Brodie by MURIEL SPARK.

Such a list contains books of very differing quality. And this is something noticeable about the trend: it is motivated so strongly by the desire to find books which will speak meaningfully and successfully to teenage reluctants that the quality of the book is often a secondary consideration. I am not suggesting that there is no criticism of the use of such books with young people. I am suggesting that it is an increasingly accepted and encouraged teaching practice. The professional journals carry articles about the ins-and-outs of such lists and books, about the use of adult novels in schools and the inclusion of them on teenage library shelves. It is happening more and more. And it is happening because there is a vacuum which must and will be filled. Teachers, librarians and parents are seeing that the young *want* books, and *will* read given the 'right' books. The argument runs that at 13 the teenager these days is so much more developed in every way than his grandparents were 'before the war', that they are ready for adult books, that there is no literature that can be specially 'theirs' as there is now a recognisable 'children's' literature. Thus the adult shelves are scoured for books that treat of the kind of topics I listed earlier, and such books as I list above are put into the hands of the young because they do this. There is a growing collection of series published by respectable educational departments which put out such novels. The most well known and one of the best is Heinemann Educational Books' New Windmill Series. As they proliferate, the danger becomes apparent. The scramble for books to keep the series going becomes more and more competitive and the net is spread wider and wider, so that inevitably the quality and 'rightness' of the books chosen declines. There is not a sufficiently large pool of suitable novels to draw on.

I am by no means persuaded that such a method is valid, or in the teenager's best interests. We all know the amusing laboratory experiment in which a vacuum is created in a can. If the can is strong enough it retains its perfect shape and the vacuum inside it. If the can is weak, it crumples and the vacuum is filled. This is precisely what I imagine happens to those youngsters – and they are the majority – who come to, or are given adult books too soon in their lives. The reading vacuum is filled, but the vessel is wounded. Sillitoe, Barstow and MacInnes, whatever we judge their quality to be, are essentially reading for experienced maturity, and, in my view, though not crippling as reading for the teenager, are certainly not books one would most wish to give reluctant readers. They explore their subjects and themes deeply, at greater length in their expository scenes than reluctant readers can often sustain, and employ a treatment best suited to people with experience of their topic and on a level of some subtlety. Far from being direct, open treatments of their themes, realistic in approach, there is often an element of satire, and of selective concentration which requires either personal knowledge of such scenes, or a developed reading power to understand and absorb them healthily. By the fact that they are reluctant readers early teenagers especially are not equipped to read such material creatively.

It is not the morality, the rawness of their language, the harshness of their style, the uninhibited choice of words and scenes that bother me. It is merely the fact that these writers are working at a level outside the present ability of most teenagers – of school age at any rate – to handle creatively. Ideally such books must be read with a sympathetic teacher to act as the stimulant, the interpreter, the catalyst to the kind of discussion which will open up such books to the reluctant reader's understanding and make him sensitive to the various elements in the texture of the books. But we are not discussing such ideal situations. (To leave aside the question of how many such capable, sympathetic teachers there are in the schools.) We are discussing the meaning and place of books in a free situation where a reader chooses his own books and reads them without required reference to an adult mind.

I would also suggest that throwing the reluctant reader into a situation where he is faced with a collection of adult books he is led to believe he will find attractive, often encourages yet again a deeper reluctance. For many young people such an experience with books produces nothing more than a time of trial selection which, by the luck of the draw and the misleading quality of the sales blurb and covers on the books, causes his selection to misfire a number of times. He then supposes that books said to deal with things which certainly catch his attention, do so at a depth, length and in a style he finds frustrating, boring, or uncompelling. Thus he is confirmed in his opinion that books are not for him. That books are misleading stuffy things. That he is in some way deficient. For after all, he sees about him adults and contemporaries who claim to enjoy and find exciting these same books. He does not understand that all that has happened is that he has been given food too strong for him, too far ahead of his present development.

The newspapers, especially the ones most popular with the majority of reluctant readers, are full of language and sensitivity debased to extremes: the commonest technique being the titillation of the appetites (any will do, but sexual ones preferred) by *double entendre*, 'news' pictures, cartoons, the selection of 'news' presented. (Vicars running off with women parishioners, starlets in divorce suits, Pop figures involved in the fashionable wickedness of the moment, and the sensationalists among criminals are the most popular, with mud-being-slung-at-politicians following as a constant secondary refrain.) None of any of this is at all helpful in creation or recreation, and little of it is news as that term was once understood by Fleet Street. The *Mirror* – for whom I have great admiration: as a technical performance it is cleverly written and presented – most popularly succeeds in the sort of journalism I hinted at when discussing boys' reading – the written-up 'story'. Donald Zec is the exponent here: he's a kind of super-Lloyd Alexander: matey with the famous, cynical, revealing, critical of them and his readers and yet admiring too, creator of the hero out of the non-heroic, slick and Americanised in style, a master-hand at direct, dialogue writing. Quite an achievement!

All this we not only leave around where young people can find it easily: we encourage them to read it. (Have you ever listened in to school staff-room conversation when things like this are said: 'It wouldn't be so bad if they read the newspapers – at least they would know what is going on!'?) Most of us read the stuff ourselves anyway – and enjoy it. Thus, even if we don't encourage them ourselves, there is precious little done to make a stand against such writing, or to reveal it for what it is. It simply does not make sense to be censorious about books like *Young Mother* and to turn a blind eye, if nothing more, to the profusion of such writing as this.

Society as a whole has engaged in such misguided thinking. Our too easy permissiveness, our disbelief in the fact that there is a right time for most things and that some things are best kept until people have grown to them – these are the root causes. We have lapsed from the knowledge that growth comes by selection, that it is encouraged by leading from the known to the unknown in steps that will not cause us to do the splits because they are so strenuous to make, that the personality must be stretched but not elasticated to the point where all ability to stretch is exhausted. We have come to recognise childhood as a time for which there is a literature worth writing, valid as a form in itself (though the deed is falling far short of the word). We have not yet come to realise that socio-cultural factors have created a similar situation in what we call 'teenage'. As John Rowe Townsend says, 'We do not help . . . by going on as though he [the teenager] either didn't exist or was a deplorable and temporary phenomenon.'

Too often criticism is made of adult books and the few trials at relevant books for teenagers, not on the lines I have suggested, but on the basis of the offensiveness of themes, language, situations, or characters. It is criticism stimulated by the critic's own prejudices, tastes, upbringing and beliefs, and as such it has its place in his opinion. But let such criticism be presented honestly as such, not as a dogmatic assertion that young people are either deeply wounded, or being corrupted by exposure to 'offensive' language and behaviour as it might be employed in their literature if a writer were to describe modern life truthfully. And let us not tie the hands of artists working directly for young people, while leaving free the hands of popular mass culture producers, as well as teachers, librarians and parents to prescribe as suitable material books, magazines, papers, films and TV programmes which unashamedly and often irresponsibly flaunt far more potentially dangerous material than any writer of quality for the young is even vaguely likely to put in front of his audience. To do so, to make such a two-faced approach to life, smacks of hypocrisy, whether conscious or not. If we censor books which honestly reveal themselves as being for teenagers by refusing to consider them for publication, for recommendation, or for fair payment as works of creative artists, then to be right and straight thinking we must do the same with even the good-quality adult fiction we now promote in the market-place of the classroom and school libraries.

I hold no brief for the deliberate inclusion of offensive material in teenage fiction; I don't even advocate the inclusion of offensive material just because it is literal truth in daily life and therefore justifiable in teenage books about life. I am here merely asking for consistent judgement and standards in our treatment of books, and all art forms we bring into the ken of the young. With that straight we might then be able to consider young people's fiction from the same standpoint as we would consider any work of art. Art is art because it selects from life; selects in such a way that we become aware of life with a clarity we might not so far have achieved, aware of life in a way the artist holds to be truthful – an expression of his personal vision of life. Art is something that increases our perceptions, makes us more sensitive, more able to see new strains in our lives, to understand what being human is all about and what the universe in which we live and move and have our being really is. Most of all it makes us able to contain ourselves in laughter and maintain ourselves in sorrow: it makes us more what we should be and better than we would be. Not better in any moralistic sense, but rather in a fuller sense, that of a mature personality living an individual life among others, and within a physical and metaphysical universe.

This is to place the discussion on a high-falutin' plane, but it is the bed-rock upon which everything else must be founded. Upon such foundations, it is nonsense to speak of anyone being harmed by a truthful reflection of things they see and hear and experience in their daily lives. It also makes nonsense of the work of writers who employ say bad language merely because it is heard in the streets, or include themes of sensational attraction merely because they happen in the streets. And it makes nonsense of the critic who cannot so contain his own prejudices and tastes that neither can he decide what is right and truthful when such things do enter a story, and what is not.

Let me take as an example of what I mean part of an incident from one of the popular adult titles, *Saturday Night and Sunday Morning*. At one point in the story we find this:

> 'Bogger you then,' he swore, and turned to walk out of the room. He changed his mind and went back, kissing her on the lips. 'Thanks,' he said. She lifted her fist to hit him, but he caught the strong wrist and stopped her. 'You touch me,' he said, 'and see what you get.' He pressed her arm back until the pain of it showed on her face. 'Let me go, you bastard,' she said. 'Somebody's coming down the yard.' He heard a knocking at the back door, and released her. The light out, they ran downstairs.
>
> 'Brenda?' Jack called out. 'Let me in. I forgot my snap.'
>
> Arthur caught hold of Em'ler and whispered: 'Keep 'im talkin'. I'm going out by the front door.'
>
> 'I'll do as I think fit,' she answered in her normally idiotic voice. 'I might keep 'im talkin' and I might not. You can't make me. It's up to me to say whether I'll do it or not, let me tell you.'
>
> 'You bastard,' Arthur hissed. 'Keep quiet.'
>
> 'I'm not a bastard,' she cried.
>
> 'All right then. But for Christ's sake don't yap so loud.'
>
> Jack hammered on the door shouting: 'Open up, Brenda. Who's in there with you?'
>
> '*You* might be a bastard,' Em'ler went on as if she hadn't heard the knocking, 'whatever your name is, but I'm not one. If you think I'm a bastard I'll show you my birth certificate to prove it.'
>
> 'You're worse,' Arthur said and left her talking and fumbling in her apron pocket as if she really did carry a birth certificate with her. (pp. 78–79 Pan edition.)

In cold out-of-context print like this such a passage stirs two prejudices of my own: a dislike of the use of the word bastard, and a strong reaction against the blasphemy against God. The one is a rational decision, the result of hearing about an illegitimate man who related the discomfort irresponsible use of the word caused him; and the other is a violent emotional objection, the result of my faith. Having cleared that ground, I would then criticise the use of such language as being unnecessary to the situation. In other words, I would want to question its selection out of all possible alternatives we really do use as bad language. If, however, we place the passage in context we find it is part of a scene in which Brenda is attempting with Em'ler's aid to 'bring off' an illegitimate pregnancy fathered by Arthur. The man at the door is Brenda's husband. The entire chapter before this incident (Chapter 6) is truthful in terms of the reportage, and skilled in the writing. Sillitoe mixes a strangely satiric sense of comedy with the horrors of such a scene which makes it, I find, terrible in its effect. (The technique is very similar to Dickens in *Oliver Twist*.) The common use of 'bastard' as Sillitoe here employs it takes on overtones which add to this effect, and the climax is reached at the lines in which God's name is used blasphemously, Our Lord's own apparent illegitimacy here adding to the tragedy of such a human predicament.

All this is true of this scene and the book as a whole. It is not a great work of literature, but it is certainly an effective and skilful one. It is also too profound in its technicalities, in the interlocking of such elements within the book for an incompetent reluctant reader to unravel unguided, and this for me makes it a questionable book to hand out indiscriminately to young people. Yet this is what has happened as a result of the filming of the book and the recommendation of it by teachers and those librarians who genuinely and desperately try to fill the vacuum.

The story concerns human situations which deeply involve young people and of which they are aware without the stimulus of this book to make them so. Yet because it is so complex a tale the effect it has might be superficial and unhealthy despite its author's honesty and quality. The story is not handled subtly enough to make it possible for an inexperienced reader to enjoy the story without being conscious of the deep disturbing themes; nor is it simply direct enough to put the resolution of those themes within his grasp.

This then is the vital danger of adult books that might be recommended, and I hope the discussion of this particular title has suggested some of the problems an author has when he begins to tackle such difficult material in books deliberately intended for the young.

None of this absolves us from trying. Rather it makes the importance of the task even more apparent. Unless we solve these problems then we can look only for a half-literate population many of whom have been deeply wounded by literature of good quality (not to mention work of poor quality) which they had handed to them far too soon.

It also leaves us in the position of having to recognise that teenage books will – *must* – include language, themes and subjects which so far receive heavy censorship at various hands, from publishers' editors at one end to parents at the other. One knows, but cannot for obvious reasons quote examples, of books which have been disgracefully savaged by publishers because the original manuscript contained language that was felt to be bothersome, not because anyone in the editorial department took exception to it for artistic or educational reasons, but because some director felt that adverse reaction from librarians would result in lower sales, and bad publicity. Such things are not uncommon, and perhaps the saddest and most appalling thing of all is that the authors of such mishandled books either have not the courage or financially cannot afford to make a stand.

At this point all I want to state is the fact that the problem of delicate subjects and offensive language is one that must be faced. Its solution lies primarily in the hands of the authors, and I will explore it in Part Two.

Footnote on the Carnegie Medal.

Since this book was written the Carnegie Medal for 1968 has been awarded to Alan Garner's *The Owl Service*. Shortly after the award was made *The Times Literary Supplement* published an article by the Chairman of the Selection Committee about the criteria and significance of the Medal. The article and the subsequent controversy further emphasise my comments.

The choice of *The Owl Service* was cheering news. It was unfortunate that Henry Treece's *The Dream-Time*, an advance in the field of historical fiction quite as important as Garner's in the field of adolescent literature, should have come in the same year and was Treece's last book before his death. Treece deserved a medal if anyone did!

The controversy began publicly at last in the *T.L.S.* is not over, and it is to be hoped it will help bring about the necessary changes in the way the Medal is chosen and presented.

PART TWO

How Write

5

The Reluctant Author

It is not difficult to find the reasons why good, competent, professional writers rarely write for teenagers, and why so few do for children. I have a file of letters from authors of experience and standing from which the following comments are taken (deliberately left without by-lines!):

> I write for fame and money (in that order), so that first I may fatten my ego and then my family can eat it. Now, there is not so much of either in [teenage books].

> I just couldn't write for so small a royalty – especially as I have a £400 overdraft at the moment!

> Many thanks for your letter. I wish I could be more eager in response. But the terms are rather on the austere side. . . .

> At present he is fully committed on his novels, and is unable to undertake any further work. (Signed, an author's agent.)

> I think the point at issue with a writer is where he places his allegiance. If it is to the craft itself, then all he can hope for is that the craft will eventually pay. And there is no knowing this, one way or the other – one hopes. If one does it for a living, then there always comes the question of compromise. The days of the garret artist are done for: even the lowest-paid hack wants a red wall-to-wall carpet. And who can blame him? Much as one bewails the fact and sometimes longs for Arcady, there is still the milkman and the baker and the Electricity Board. Then there's the things one sees want doing: such as teenage books, and all that can be scraped together are intending writers who are teachers, and longing for the laurel-wreath and a photo in the Observer Colour Supplement. It'll always be the same, I'm afraid. I had a talk with a publisher last week that would make your ears shrivel and drop off. Mine almost did. One comes away with a sick at heart feeling, that soon smoulders into something like revenge.

Need I go on? Every one of these extracts comes from a successful, well-known professional fiction writer. And the final sentence of the last one ('. . . a sick at heart feeling, that soon smoulders into something like revenge') states graphically the situation as it exists too often between the author and the publisher, as any reading of the professional magazines which air the topic will prove. Beneath the gloss and sparkle of the lunch-occasion photographs, behind the hand-shakes and the published successes of the book business, lie battle-grounds of charred relationships and animosities created by the author–publisher commercial rat-race. There are notable exceptions, men and women devoted to their work as authors and publishers. On both sides there are also too many who are third rate in every way, scrambling to eat the pickings each claim to be theirs.

Thus in an area of publishing and authorship which is uncertain, even untried – the teenage 'market' – there is caution, scepticism, fearfulness. What books should be written? How should they be marketed? What are the returns likely to be? Anyone who writes for young people between 11 and 16 does so because they either must, want to try, or can't find any other audience they can succeed with (the 'intending writers . . . longing for the laurel-wreath'). I want to let some of the better ones speak for themselves, in the hope that what they have to say might help writers who want to write young people's books, and that out of the horse's mouth, so to speak, might come ideas relevant to our topic.

Reginald Maddock first. He is an experienced children's author, a schoolmaster of maturity, and a man who knows reluctant readers of all kinds, and the less intelligent ones especially. His book *The Pit* strikes me as being of a very fine quality, and is certainly much read by my own reluctant readers.

> There are those who resist reading because reading is something adults make them do. Unless they are young children, their reluctance does not necessarily spring from lack of ability. They may be young in years – 12+ onwards – but they are often old in experience. They no longer believe in Santa Claus or fairies. Reading's for squares. They've tried it and it does nothing for them. The books they read as children – because they are forced to read them – are about artificial worlds nothing like the real world their young lives are lived in. Teachers and parents may get their kicks and fantasies from books but they know easier ways of getting them more swiftly. I write at times for children like this. I try to write about real kids with real problems similar to their own. I write about bullies, hooligans, vandals; about juvenile crime, unsympathetic adults, drunken or careless parents, unenlightened teachers, truancy, homework, etc. These are the things they know about. These are the characters they identify with.

Maddock's experience here matches my own. Yet I have a letter from a leading children's editor commenting about a book like one of Reginald Maddock's, who says: 'It has been our experience, however, confirmed by that of booksellers and librarians, that children do not really want this kind of realism in their books.'

Now there's a thing! Someone somewhere is wrong. I'd agree they don't like or want it *all the time*. My own experience as a boy and as a teacher-librarian supports Maddock and not the publisher or the advisers.

Maddock goes on:

> Many of these children never made the transition from children's books to adult books because there is nothing for them to read except cadet editions and bowdlerised books so emasculated that they no longer satisfy. I refer now to children who, by some miracle, have not in their early years built up a resistance to reading. They would go for James Bond and Mickey Spillane, but who encourages them to read such books and where is the writer who has succeeded in writing for *them*? There isn't one, because the few who have tried, and I am one of them, have been stopped in their tracks by publishers. Publishers draw a line between children and adults and recognise no intermediate stage, largely because to publish books for adolescents is a doubtful starter financially.

What Reginald Maddock says is reflected also in an article printed in the 17 October 1964 edition of *The Bookseller*. Robert J. Hoare wrote of his experiences as a children's writer before he gave it up for textbooks, on which he does very nicely thank you. He had written a series of children's thrillers with a central character who appeared for the first time in 1958 in *Robby to the Rescue*. Nice things were said by all the reviewing magazines concerned with children's books: Hoare understood what he was doing and did it competently. Eventually, however, he:

> . . . brought the ROBBY series to a premature conclusion, not without some regret. I liked writing for children, I liked writing these adventure stories. Believe it or not it wasn't primarily the financial aspect that ended my brief career as an author of children's fiction. It was also the sheer frustration of knowing that the books were not getting through to the children for whom they were intended. The other day I attended a meeting at which a teacher-librarian and a children's librarian discussed with children's authors various aspects of the subject in which they were all interested. One fact emerged strikingly. Too many children today do not have a love of books. Too many children are not habitual readers. Too few children read books for the pure unalloyed pleasure of reading them. Between the children's books that teachers and librarians condemn (e.g. Enid Blyton banned from Nottingham libraries recently and W. E. Johns, I am informed, excluded from at least one place) and the books they recommend ('You *must* read Rosemary Sutcliff', they gush to a 10-year-old boy with an I.Q. of 95, a reading age of about 10.0, a father who has the telly on all night, and a home without a hard-backed book in it) – between these there is a broad no-man's land. It is nonsense to say that books to fill this no-man's land are not available. They are. The trouble is they are not bought by the people who control the purse strings.
>
> If you take the trouble to look back over *unselective* lists of books for children published in the last ten years, you will note among the authors many who no longer write children's books. Many of them have graduated to writing adult books; some have transferred to the field of school text-books; some, I suppose, have simply found other outlets than writing for their extra-curricular activities.

When I say that I nearly became a children's author, I know that I am not alone.

The no-man's land of teenage books, poor payment for the work, and the frustration of success because of the established ideas about what children like, should have or need, so that the books do not reach the audience they were intended for: these things come keenly alive from the comments I've so far quoted, and these truthfully reflect what is often said by authors who have written or might write young people's books.

One author who has succeeded brilliantly in creating a continuing popular audience for his books, and the support – grudging sometimes, but support nevertheless – of the librarians is Malcolm Saville. I've heard him lumped with Blyton and Johns, and dissociated from the denigration these two top of the Pops receive only by such words as: 'He's better than them, of course.' I was keen to hear what Saville had to say, because he is a prolific writer, and one who is attempting to find a market among the adolescents with his Simon Baines books which Heinemann publish. His Lone Pine stories run into sixteen titles, which almost qualifies him as one of those series writers I criticised earlier. Certainly his books are enormously popular with my own reluctants.

When the 15th Lone Pine appeared in 1964, Rosemary Manning reviewed it and the general panorama of Saville's 20-year-long span of work in an article published in the *Teacher* for 24 July 1964. It would repay searching out by the specialist. The review is favourable, indeed almost nostalgic (perhaps Miss Manning was once a Lone Piner herself) and can be summed up in this comment: '. . . generous acknowledgement should be made to novels like Malcolm Saville's: workmanlike, readable, and engrossing.'

As a successful story-teller, a series writer, and a craftsman with over twenty years of work behind him, I felt Saville ought to have a say. I asked him several questions relevant to our topic, hoping he would be as frank and honest as he liked. He was not only this: he was also painstaking and generous in his answer to my request, as in fact were most of the writers I contacted. Here are some of the things he said:

> I am not aware of any particular difficulty in writing for 12+. This doesn't mean that I find any of my writing easy – far from it. I try to invent a plot and write the sort of story I should have enjoyed myself. I do not delude myself that I have a mission. I suppose it is true that in all my fiction I try to please myself first. In *everything* I write I know that I have failed unless I can make the reader want to read on.

It seems to me that there could hardly be a better statement of what makes a good competent author for any age than this. It reveals the secret – in so far as it was ever secret – of Saville's popularity.

Saville then went on to answer my criticisms of the series writer and the critics who mention Saville himself in the same breath as Blyton–Johns.

> I do not know who it is who lumps me with other popular writers. Who are these critics? Teachers? Librarians who like telling children what they want them to read?
>
> Editors who haven't been able to get a popular series writer on their lists?
>
> I'm used to not being mentioned. I'm more or less used to being ignored by the self-appointed critics. [Saville goes on to list these!]
>
> I'll tell you a true story. Nearly 20 years ago when I was beginning to be a modest success with Lone Pine, I was approached by another editor to do another series. As I was already being copied by another popular writer I agreed and this second series, *The Jillies*, is still selling well in paperback. When we got the second of these out which was a good original story I was barely mentioned although it was broadcast in a B.B.C. Children's Hour serial. I commented on this to my editor – about the best I have ever worked with – and I shall never forget his answer. 'You're too innocent and if you aren't careful you'll get hurt. You are now a success and the wolves will be after you. It will never again be the same for you. Your work will be plagiarised and even if you notice, it won't be worth taking action. Your titles will be copied. Other 'first time' authors will use your idea of a genuine background and even the same places will be used. You will become both prolific and popular and the only people who will love you are your readers and your publishers.'
>
> All this has come true, and now we have this nonsense about series. Of course I believe in them! They are a wonderful way of encouraging young people to read and to enjoy books – and even to buy them. It is monstrous to suggest that 'popular' series writers are morally at fault because they write to please their readers. What is the good of writing books that only a few children want to read? NO! This country is raising a generation at colossal cost which regards books as a luxury and something to be borrowed rather than bought and treasured. It is a generation which is finding it immensely difficult to communicate because it isn't really literate, although it may be clever. It is non-literate because some parents think reading is a waste of time and because of some exhausted, frustrated and disillusioned teachers. Behind this is a State system which doesn't appear to believe it important to spend more money to pay more dedicated teachers for the PRIMARY schools where the young should be, and usually are, encouraged to appreciate books. Don't blame the series writer for 'reluctant readers' – be thankful for the few who are showing children that they can actually read for pleasure.

Apart from Saville's argument for the series, what strikes me in what he says is his energetic critique of the system that has made reluctant readers. A man who has never taught, always been involved in book production (for many years he was a publisher's editor) and a successful popular children's author, by his own experience has been forced into precisely the same position about the causes of reluctance as I found myself in Part One of this book.

And on top of this, he gives a graphic picture of the hazards of popular authorship. Any author who stands for other than Carnegie Medal standards as I have analysed them and becomes successful must look out for precisely the treatment Malcolm Saville describes.

But Saville is very much a children's author. His comment on the themes I listed earlier was: 'I wouldn't be particularly keen to write novels for young people on the sort of themes you mention because I am not sure I could do it well enough.'

Joan Tate is a writer I have mentioned a number of times before. She strikes me as being talented and yet also very astute in her work for reluctant readers. Her *Joan Tate Books* (Heinemann Educational Books) are enormously successful. Her book *Sam and Me* (Pan-Macmillan Topliners) is one of the few books I know which I would suggest as the beginnings of a genuine, quality teenage fiction.

She described to me how she came to write for the submerged 60 per cent (a term she gave me):

> My main impression of reading material for the young of this age was that there wasn't any. My own young – all readers of varying intelligence – found there was practically nothing for them but Agatha Christie and Monica Dickens and so on at 12, 13, 14 age. Nothing. Except the usual children's historical novels which they disliked because they only too soon saw that it was an adult's way of escaping the issue of presenting life to them. You've only got to look down the list of books by really good writers for children to see how many of them are historical fiction or adventure stories set outside this country and of a totally unreal nature. In this, writers are of course not alone – our whole education system took this line until recently. Librarians are often the worst – 'They aren't interested' – I've heard this said of children over and over again – without a second's thought that perhaps it might be the other way round – that the books were not interesting.
>
> My own books came from repeated remarks that there were no books for the young who *didn't* read, rather than couldn't. So I sat down and wrote the first two, keeping the story simple with virtually one character, the English good but clear and simple, the background essentially everyday and ordinary, outside school life. The idea – if it can be called that – was that brevity and swiftness of style and short-ness of the book, would keep the reluctant reader going out of sheer interest – I hoped – and then the delight of the reading would have taken the first step. Once you get the young reading, you can't stop them, and then it remains to get them to sort out the good from the bad in their own minds.
>
> The reviews of my books talk about how well they have been cut (they haven't), the carefully constructed sentences (they aren't), their moral strength, elegance of plot and all that sort of gumph, but miss the real point, which is that they are true (the best of them, anyhow) in the proper literary sense in that they reflect life, but they are still just stories. So you see, I haven't really any 'principles' on the subject, except that as long as writing is genuine, it will be acceptable to the young, and also a conviction that adolescence and its difficulties, particularly in human relationships,

is something that happens to all of us, wherever we come from, and we all tend to forget it, if possible, or at least try to ignore it.

Joan Tate's remarks are worth exploring. First, and probably most important, she reinforces what needs hammering home: the essential quality of the reading for reluctants is a compelling story, and goes on to make the point that no scissors-and-paste technique can achieve a book of value. Her books have not been cut, or her sentences carefully constructed in an educational sense, and all the things she dismisses as 'gumph'; not because they aren't necessary, but because her preparation for the job made these things instinctive to her work. And this is where the intending writer, and the publisher's editor who thinks young people's books can be made by a policy statement and contract in one hand, and a pair of scissors supported by a pot of glue in the other, both go wrong. Joan Tate had behind her, as a background to the books she first wrote, years of varied experience, among other things some somewhat unorthodox teaching of English to young people regarded as 'no good', a great deal of teaching of English to adolescent foreign students of all intelligence levels, whose reading problems are very similar to those of our reluctant reader, a practical, ear-sizzling knowledge of the world of young people's clubs, and a family of her own. She had also had some years of experience in a totally different writing world, that of journalism, broadcasting, reading and translation – a fact which must have contributed to a certain clarity and lucidity in her writing. She herself, a reading addict, and her own children, discarded traditional children's books as 'without meat, strength or even interest' at a very early age indeed – long before the age of 10 for which so many so-called 'junior novels', in fact simply longer 'children's' books, are designated by publishers, and she is convinced that a great many children do this and thus soon lose the habit of reading acquired when younger. Children do not 'lose interest' in books at a certain age, she says – the books are no longer interesting to them, and she is convinced that the adult world has grossly underestimated the maturity of children's minds, largely because the young are so very often so inarticulate when it comes to explaining *why* they like or dislike something, and adults are not often prepared to listen to them, and also it is always adults who choose their books for them. She also has theories, now put successfully into practice in Sweden, on the teaching of our language to young people who come from homes in which language, as such, is scarcely ever used – and this applies equally to an English home where television and a rushed life have reduced conversation to a minimum, as it does to a Swedish home in which English as a language is seldom, if ever, heard. Given, she says, a level of language which they can cope with, a swift story of a length that is not too daunting, youngsters will read about anything, but will be more than just interested if the story bears some relation to his or her life as it is, and is going to be in the near future. Her talent (whatever 'talent' is) is strong. And she finds living exciting. Ordinary living: not some fantasy world bred by an escape into her own imagination. Because of all this, when she comes to write a book in the way she describes, she naturally, without contrivance, writes the sort of book needed for reluctant readers.

Besides all this, before she sets pen to paper, she goes through the stages which every writer of any worth must experience: she spends a good deal of time, sometimes six months, thinking through her story, handling it in her imagination. Too many of the books which appear on the market, the 'good' books selected by 'discriminating readers' as well as those neglected by them, bear painful signs of having been finished even before this essential work was begun. Their stories lack compulsion and energy because they were never tested in the author's imagination: they were cerebrally conceived and mechanically manipulated while they were written, their author unmoved by anything he set down in words.

Unless all these things are so: experience of the audience, practice, a time when the story is absorbed into the imagination, and then at last the actual process of writing: then compromise is likely to mar the story, faulting the book. An interesting example of this is John Rowe Townsend's *Gumble's Yard*.

The heart of this attractive novel, one of my Five Star titles, is how a family of children in a 'depressed' home and area cope with the situation when their parents desert. Worked into this thread of the plot is another of the cops-and-robbers kind. One feels that this was a compromise on the part of the author, made because he thought his story needed such popular appeal to succeed commercially. Certainly, the story has a duality about it: the two themes never quite merge. The concession is an understandable one, but it is nevertheless one which mars the book. Nor, in my view, was it a necessary concession: his major theme is appealing to young people, and handled extraordinarily well.

I have already mentioned the same author's book *Hallersage Sound*, and suggested that the use of the Pop group as a central part of the plot leaves a lot to be desired. That book and others which attempt to approach teenage fiction in the same way throw up a number of interesting comments on the author's situation.

First, the present problem of most children's writers, especially the established, middle-aged and older ones, is their age. Not their physical age, but their social age. Teenage being what now it has become, I think it is doubtful if anyone who has not lived through the 'teenage' culture – something that has really only been what it now is for the last twenty years at most – can cope in imaginative literature with sufficient sympathetic conviction and knowledge to lend his work that verisimilitude young people look for in their reading. It demands, from those who have not experienced it, an imaginative leap quite beyond the power of most people: and it requires knowledge both of the culture and the young to a degree many writers would not be prepared to give themselves.

This will pass, and in the next few years maybe there will emerge writers with plenty to say, and with a knowledge of young people's culture gained through direct living experience during their own days as teenagers. Then we might well get the books we need.

Granted writers who can, they must still be persuaded to do. And if Aunt Jemima still rules the roost both as buyer and as editor then no such writer will even give the opportunity and the need a second's consideration. Young people's books must be a field in which the writer does not feel he will have his talents stifled or even less well rewarded. We need to push out the barriers. But this is not as simple a matter as it sounds. Here is Josephine Kamm, writing about *Young Mother* in a letter answering my queries about the effect possible rejection of the book had on her while writing it:

> I was indeed inhibited by the knowledge that if I dealt as frankly with the subject as I wished no publisher would touch it. I felt strongly that a book on the subject was needed, even one which of necessity left much unsaid; and I hoped that once the ice had been broken with a book on illegitimacy franker books might be written. At the moment this seems unlikely because, as I think you know, *Young Mother* has been banned in certain quarters.

The answer to this problem concerns many different professional book people in many different ways, and these ways I have tried to deal with under appropriate headings elsewhere. The answer for the author is to compromise as little as he can, but it is also deeper and more far-reaching than this.

In the first place, I doubt whether young people's books will ever come, in the main, from children's writers of standing. Such writers are ingrained with habits, thought forms, even attitudes to the requirements of the children's book. The true teenage book cuts across many of these things. I would rather expect the good teenage writers to come from the young writers now emerging as competent adult writers, and, as at present in children's books, from writers who feel that this is their proper field of work: they are attracted by it, or find themselves able to communicate with young people of this age better than any other, and do this by choice for all their writing lives or for part of them. But, as everyone points out, at present there is no recognised teenage literature, and there is no feeling among writers and publishers that it is a field of valid activity at all. So this ends up a publisher's problem, and will be discussed in Chapter 9.

Next, writers of the kind needed will not compromise with Aunt Jemima. In America this seems to have happened. There is in the States a very highly developed business in Y.A.'s – Young Adults' books. And these books sell. Yet on the whole they are sickeningly unreal. They have compromised so far that the realities of the people they claim to deal with have little to do with the stories they tell. It would be sad if a similar situation grew up here, and there are signs that it might. (Marjorie Gayler's books follow this trend; and there is a slowly growing number of books of this kind imported from the States and published here.) Jay Williams, an American author of books for children and adults, analysed it for me like this:

> I was very interested in your comments on American children's books. Yes, I think you are right – there is a coating of sentimentality over most novels for kids here, which is part of the American spirit. The books are written by grown-ups, most of whom are parents, and they reflect (no matter how carefully the writer might try to the contrary) a wistful desire to have kids behave towards parents as the writer wishes his own kids to behave towards him. On the other hand, however, remember that a lot of this reflects reality – the relationship between parents and children *is* different from the English. As far as the activity between the sexes goes, what you have read only reflects the American notion of how activity between the sexes *ought* to look. We are struggling here between our Puritanical roots and an accelerating degeneration in sexual morals. Our kids can buy, on any newsstand, quite freely, the dirtiest books ever written. Our incidence of dope-peddling in the high schools is frightening. Our numbers of teenage pregnancies are increasing. But we can't put this into books for kids, because no one would publish them, and the schools and libraries, which account for most book sales, wouldn't touch them. However, there *are* some good, honest books about teenage love, written by people like Betty Cavanna, for instance, which my daughter finds enormously to her taste and which all her friends read avidly. And also you must understand that of the hundreds and hundreds of titles which appear every year here the vast majority are written by women who are not professional writers. Not professional in the sense that although they may write several or more books, they are married and rely on their husbands for support. They treat the income from their books as a welcome dollop of gravy, and use it to buy the nice things they couldn't otherwise afford. They don't have to live on it. It means their attitude towards their work can be more self-indulgent. They don't write because they are driven to it willy-nilly, but because it is a pleasant avocation, a supplement to bridge clubs and community work. And profitable.

Jay Williams' last sentence explains why there are so many books for young people in the States. An earlier one – 'but we cannot put all this into books for kids because no one would publish them' – explains why so few of them are written by writers of worth.

We can, then, do without the gap-filler, the paste-and-scissors editorial writer (common mostly in Educational Publishers' lists), the moral do-gooder who writes for 'purpose', and the profitable hobbyist. It's the willy-nilly writer we want, the one who can't help himself: he just MUST write.

For him certain things will be true. (All other things being equal with other branches of publishing – things like payment, recognition, and opportunity to publish.) First, he might be a teenage writer anyway, as some writers feel they are children's writers. I believe they exist but haven't come to light because there is little publishing opportunity and recognition for them. Secondly, an adult writer might well feel that a particular story can best be told in the way that appeals most to teenagers: it has the qualities that appeal to this age, and the story demands that form. For this reason Steinbeck's *The Pearl* and *The Red Pony* make excellent young people's books, though in fact they are not deliberately intended to be so. Their theme, treatment and length are exactly right. Which brings us to the third avenue for the creation of teenage literature: the work of an adult writer, which without his deliberately intending it as such, makes the teenage audience the best one for that particular book.

Very, very few writers of real talent and inspiration count themselves children's writers: the great children's books have come mostly from writers whose real work and intention lay in other, usually adult directions. If there are few children's writers like this, there are fewer still who would count themselves teenage writers. One author of real talent and potential, however, who does seem to look at himself in this way is Alan Garner. Garner has written four books in ten years. The first, *Weirdstone of Brisingamen*, appeared in 1960; its sequel, *The Moon of Gomrath*, in 1963; *Elidor* in 1965; and *The Owl Service* in 1967. *The Owl Service* was sold out of its first impression only a month or so after publication. It caused flutters in many dovecotes, received an unusual and not entirely unanimous press, and was one of the very few books to have been published under the stigma of an 'older children's book' to receive serious comment on the adult review page of a national paper. *The Sunday Times* gave it space among the adult novels, calling it 'a major experience'. Few people at the time realised what six months later was being accepted: *The Owl Service* is a milestone, a turning-point in children's books, and young people's books especially.

Garner makes concessions to no one. He writes to please himself, because he must. His integrity is already a legend among the 'in' people of publishing circles, and some people see in him a writer who has the artistic power, and the right qualities and experience to create young people's books of such worth that neglect of them will be impossible by anyone, either of the old guard or the new. His books demand attention. The last two also have a strange, compelling effect on even the most reluctant reader.

Let me describe two occasions on which Garner's work had a dynamic effect on reluctant readers.

The first involves Stephen. A modern school fourth-year boy of some intelligence, he was placed in a poor stream for his last year at school. He wasn't staying on to sit the C.S.E. exam, and so he was not allowed to stay with his companions with whom he had spent the rest of his school life, but had to join the 'leavers' class: a collection of various spirits, the common factor being their date of exit. Stephen's mother and father had separated a few months earlier. Stephen had remained with his mother but had, after a few weeks, gone over to his father. This was not exactly in his own best interest. The entire situation was not one conducive to reading, especially to a boy who, throughout his school life, had complained about 'books'.

During an early library lesson with Stephen, I held up *Elidor* and said it was a book I thought some of the class might enjoy, that I didn't like that kind of book usually, but that this one had held me, and even frightened me in places. Stephen laughed derisively.

'O.K.,' I said. 'You try it.'

It was a challenge without much hope, thrown out more in self-defence than with any real idea of his accepting. (*Elidor*'s jacket is very much one for a children's book, something Stephen would normally have scorned.) However, at the end of the lesson he came up to me and said,

'Give us it, then.'

He took the book home. Next morning, twenty minutes before school opened, I found him in the library waiting for me – he was out of bounds, for that time of day, and if caught by the old guard would have risked punishment.

'I've finished it,' he said, and grinned. 'You're right! It got that bad last night I didn't dare go on, so I got up early this morning and finished it then.' He paused. 'It isn't half good,' he said.

Within two lessons he had promoted the book so well among 4c that I had to make a visit to the bookseller for extra copies. *The Owl Service* riveted him even more.

The second incident involves *The Owl Service*. Philippa Pearce, in a review of the book published in *Children's Book News* No. 4, July–August 1967, wrote:

> . . . properly to understand what is going on [in the book] the reader needs every aid: the publisher's explanatory blurb, the endpaper design of the owl plate, the author's acknowledgements and three quotations before the story begins – and the Fourth Branch [of the Mabinogion]. Even with these, the narrative power of the book may be the undoing of the susceptible reader, hurrying him on in headlong excitement towards a total of mental confusion. . . . My repeated objection, however, is not that young readers (and adults too for that matter) may understand too much, but that they are likely to understand too little. This is a great pity in a story by Alan Garner. (p. 165.)

I had read *The Owl Service* twice when I found these comments, and thought them then patent nonsense. I don't think so now: I know so. I did two things: I gave the book to some teenage reluctants to read for themselves, and at the same time read it aloud to the same 4c who found *Elidor*. Deliberately, I explained nothing. After a chapter or two, I felt the need to show them the end-paper drawings of the dinner service. At no time did I even remember the other 'aids'. The book carried 4c along in such a way that I had to handle a demand for readings from it at every English lesson. Nor was this solely the skill with which Garner can tell a story. This basic ability he has in quantity. I also found to my astonishment that several people in the class had worked out the implications of the relationships, and the paralleling of the Mabinogion tale well before I had done so in my own first reading. They had done this intuitively, led to it by the emotional power of the writing. The book fascinated them, and until this fascination had been satiated by blanket readings of Garner it ran fever-pitch and strong. And was contagious.

It seemed to me that Garner was working in the most difficult, least attractive field of young people's books, but by his skill and passion was able to bring his books alive to an astonishing extent; and he seems to make most sense when he is dealing with his adolescent characters. This is the relevant thing for me. *The Owl Service* is, whatever else it *appears* to be, a book about adolescents and the power of their unguarded loves and hates. In fact, at the time of publication, only *The Times Educational Supplement* really got to the kernel of the author's intention: their reviewer wrote (in the edition for 25 August 1967): 'The presentation of a complex psychological theme to *children no older than the characters in the story* is handled with subtle mastery, owing much to the author's recognition and understanding of adolescence.' (My italics.)

This, but this, is all we have been talking about in my weak attempt to define teenage literature. Garner does so much more so well: he demonstrates it, shows it in action. He is rewarded by the kind of results I have tried to describe in the incidents involving Stephen and 4c. He has shown that books for young people can be as honest as they demand to be, as profound as the author wishes them to be, and always of the highest quality of workmanship: he has shown they can be all this and yet still be popular, effective with the reluctant as well as with the bookish. He demonstrates what happens when the basic qualities of the show-businessman, and the willy-nilly, I-can't-help-it writer who works from an inward compulsion are fused in one talent.

The Owl Service was interesting not because it is a perfect book – it isn't: the explicit intrusion into the story of the Fourth Branch of the Mabinogion is, to my mind, a weakness in the book, rather than a strength. The book's strengths, however, indicate clearly Garner's potential as an enormously talented writer. And it was these strengths which so riveted 4c and are strong indications of what makes a true 'teenage' book. For *The Owl Service* contains much to damn it in their eyes. It is uncompromising in language, pared down in construction and narrative almost to the point where the reader is confused, and has an ending so unusual in modern children's literature (and yet so logical in context of this book) that many critics have been bemused and disturbed by it.

Nothing would seem to be further from the kind of story reluctant readers of whatever intelligence would find attractive. Yet one saw the proof that just the opposite was the case. Watching 4c's reactions in the classroom as reading followed reading, one came to understand something of the fascination of the book.

The dialogue, the main vehicle of the story, is superb: it is accurate, full of the character who speaks it, contemporary, entirely pertinent. It drives the story ineluctably on, without digression, and is never used to mouth ideas or words outside the context of the plot or character. It is, too, full of humour. Teenage books must possess such qualities to succeeed with reluctant readers.

The incidents involving the three young people together, such as the moment when Gwyn and Alison are up the mountain (Chapters 16 and 17); the taunting of Gwyn by Roger (Chapter 20); these strike deep with young people because they are such accurately recorded moments of reality in the lives of people that age. The relationship between Gwyn and his mother Nancy, and the argument they have are compelling too for the same reason. It is such things as these, apart from his technical ability, which point up Garner's talent. He has a knowledge of and a sympathy for the adolescent rare in mature adults.

The final, and probably most important element in this book, I can only describe as passion. It is that quality which works instinctively through the guts rather than the head: it lives, D. H. Lawrence would have said, in the solar plexus. Garner works on the nerves: on the feelings and sensitivities, rather than on the cerebral centres of one's being. And he intends to. This is to my mind what lies at the crux of the problem under discussion. On the whole, children's and young people's books (the ones I've so far described as 'bookish') work cerebrally: they place their emphasis on verbal awareness, on intellectually satisfying plot patterns, descriptions and narrative: they avoid exploring those things which move the blood and excite the nerves. Such books are preferred by the students of literature because they are given to intellectual analysis and understanding: it would be easier, for example, to unravel and write a critique of the work of Rosemary Sutcliff than it would of Alan Garner. Thus, critics like Philippa Pearce can write that children are 'likely to understand too little' of *The Owl Service*. She means that they will not be able to put into cold words a description of the theme, plot and characters, and the movement of the relationships between the characters, as one might in other, less 'passionate' books.

If one approaches *The Owl Service* receptively with one's feelings, however, one understands it completely. 4c did just this. It is the way they approach everything they read, because that is the kind of people they are. And I suspect it is the kind of people most people are: they are probably the submerged 60 per cent. They had seen the relationship between Huw and Nancy long before I understood it in my own first reading. And they felt the power and rightness of the end intensely. Yes, they wanted to read the book for themselves to explore it further, to understand it more consciously, and so they borrowed the book privately and read the story again. But there was none of the neurotic puzzlement that so many of the bookish critics exhibited when the book first appeared. And they were far less bothered by the 'illegitimacy and adultery, jealousy and revenge' which so bothered Miss Pearce. Why should they be? These things surround them every day and are shouted at them from every newspaper and TV set. Whether Gwyn would have the strength and the courage to do what they saw had to be done was of much more concern to them than the everyday material from which the story had been hewn. Folk-tales are, after all, only folk-tales while they deal in such matters; why should they or anyone else be more bothered by a modern folk-tale than they are by one written hundreds of years ago?

It is Garner's ability to weave a story that moves us – moves in the glorious old-fashioned sense of the word – wherein lies his real stature. And it is a rare ability. When he finally comes, as I'm sure he must, to write a novel un-encumbered by 'fantasy' or directly used sources like the Mabinogion, he will, I'm sure, write a book that engages the reluctant reader completely, not because it has been written 'for' them, but because he uses his art in the way that transcends literary, bookish formulas and standards.

I persuaded Garner to speak directly about his work. He is articulate and speaks only for himself, but a lot of what he says, it seems to me, bears keenly on the problem of writing for young people. I want to quote him at some length because also his remarks are a fascinating record of the making of his books.

> Well, to answer your treacherously simple questions ('Where are you going, and what happens if you find you are no longer a children's writer?'):
>
> In a sense, I don't know where I'm going until I'm well on the way there. 'Well on the way' means different things with different books. Sometimes the point is reached before the writing is far advanced; sometimes not. For instance, *Elidor* took two years from first conscious thought to finished manuscript, and the writing was spread fairly evenly over the period. This caused a crisis, when, having finished the book, I saw the development of two years' experience telescoped into a four hour read – The writing and style changed completely and there was no overall texture to the book. It was beyond me to cure this efficiently, and I still find that the book is in two lumps, Ch. 1–6 and Ch. 7–20. For the curious, Chapter 4 took five months of unbroken slogging to manoeuvre into place – and I don't want that again! Naturally it never will be wholly right.
>
> *The Owl Service* was four years, but all the writing happened in the last year. There was an initial burst of twelve weeks, which took the thing as far as pg 43, when I realised that, although the frame of the book was still valid, far more of me was going into it, and the texture was about to change – that is, the story was going to bite far more deeply than I had imagined. So there was then a four month period of coming to terms with this new dimension; after which the whole of the rest of the book came in eight weeks straight. Nothing like this had happened before. It was like listening to a tape recorder. Each day I sat down, picked up a pen, switched on, and listened. The result was that the overall form of the book cohered in a way that my normally painful word-hewing never had done before. Of course there were discrepancies between the original conception and the result, but my editor sent me a reader's comment which gave me the objectivity to spot what was wrong, and putting it right took hardly any time at all, say, three hours.
>
> The questions are even worse than I imagined! Where am I going? Yes. In spite

of all the above, I never know the answer with individual books: they're not planned in detail. There are certain key thoughts/incidents, and usually the end of the book presents itself as a clear cameo almost before the other ideas form, but the telling of the story is something that happens as we go along. It's as much a discovery for me as it is for the reader. If it were all coldly planned I'd never get through the manual labour of the writing. This is not to say that the story can be undisciplined. The very tightest control must be kept on technique and construction always. You must know what is happening, what has happened and what is likely to happen, but within the framework of the discipline there must be room for curiosity to play. Mind you, I think the subconscious knows very well what it is about, and I've had to learn to rely on it, once the computer has been programmed.

I think it worth reminding ourselves that Alan Garner has been a *full-time* practitioner of his art since he was in his early twenties; that he stuck to it in the early days before a penny was coming in, surviving as best he could, and well before anyone took him up. When he speaks of months he means what he says, not what the part-timer means: a few spare hours a few evenings a week. Garner means every day of every month, and this gives us a graphic idea of what is asked of anyone who wishes to turn out more than competent work.

Garner followed the above remarks by these:

> I believe that a writer is a writer; not a children's writer, not a 'fantasy writer', not even a poet, a novelist, or a playwright. Simply a writer – someone who casts words into the most efficient mould for his purpose. So, on this level, I'm a children's writer because Collins decide to put me on their children's list.
>
> Yet I do want children to read the books, and especially do I want adolescents to find them. Simply, children make the best audience. Connect with a child and you really connect. Adolescence is the same only more so. Is it 'a phase we all go through, dear', or is that the carapaced sensitivity of the adult shying away from the memory of his own awareness, an awareness that hurt so much it grew this shell? I feel that, in adolescence, we all have our chance, but that for most the beauty hurts too much. We can't stay exposed. Yet when we see it in our own children we can't cope with the memory of what might have been, if. I don't know whether this is true, and it will be some years yet before I can test it with my own children.
>
> It is this thesis, that adolescence may be a form of maturity from which the adult declines, that involves me and will do so for as far ahead as I can see. After that, if there has been progression, there will be areas of concern which I can't see for the present foothills. If these are of interest to children, then I shall still be writing for children. If not, not.
>
> Now to answer your more general questions.
>
> 'Delicate' subjects not allowed. What subjects?
>
> Who 'allows' or doesn't? And on what authority? No; kids' books are subject to the law of obscenity, along with the rest of the English language, and to no other. What schoolmaster, librarian or publisher has ever spelled out the subjects not allowed? None. It's merely creeping precedent at work: and the same process can be turned to the good. *If* there are the writers. They will have to be writers of high technical ability, and (perhaps the hardest) free from cant themselves: and honest,

above all. By 'honest', I mean that they must be able to handle the material artistic-ally: and by 'artistically', I mean that they must present it truthfully and as an integral part of its context. Not because the writer thinks, 'Ha!'

Offensive language. This is most easily expounded in a consideration of the use of 'bad' language in print. But the argument can be applied to the whole. It is inartistic simply to play back on to the page an unedited piece of a tape recording. There is no justification in saying that it must be O.K. because that's what the people said. If A talks to B and uses an obscenity, it has gone by the time that B registers it, and the emotional charge of the word(s) is dissipated, with the result that the obscenity, in conversation, is really no more than a form of signalling, a punctuation, a sign that the speaker wishes to focus attention on this piece of information. Swearwords are emotional italics in a spoken context.

Or the signposts of an inadequate mind in need of a vocabulary.

So: A uses obscenities in his conversation with B either because he wants to exaggerate, point up, aspects of his communication, or because his vocabulary is not capable of abstract expression: he can't move in three dimensions verbally: he can't qualify information.

The situation is completely altered when the words are fixed on a page. Let's take heating as an analogy. The spoken word is as efficient as a coal fire in an open hearth, with no curtains at the windows, in a house with a thin slate roof. The written word is oil-fired central heating, double-glazed windows, and fibreglass in the loft. The energy goes round and round and can't dissipate. Therefore, in re-creating A's con-versation with B, we have to convey NOT the words, but the entire emotional temperature. The obscenity that flew by is now plonk, fixed, and will destroy the context. We are not policemen reporting what the witness said. We are presenting something much more complicated.

And if we are dealing, in A, with the second case – the inadequate mind in need of a vocabulary – the job becomes much harder. Simply to turn out A's use of the same word in every possible grammatical form would be to render the thing in-comprehensible. A, as a person, would never emerge, nor would his thoughts. Golding's *The Inheritors* is the classic example of how to go about the problem.

You see, we're not dealing with swearwords, but with attitudes and people. The words of a language are to be used to this end, and if an obscenity is the way to do it, then it's O.K.: but we must be very careful to shun the day when we clink our glasses because offensive language has been published if our delight is *merely* that of getting 'sod' on to a children's list. This is where D. H. Lawrence was up the creek. Lady C. is a perfect demonstration of my argument. He ruins what could have been passages of great beauty by his misuse of vocabulary. He was intelligent enough, if he'd been honest (instead of hurt), to have realised that there are words that can't be drained of their emotional charge, nor should they be. We *need* them!

All this waffle applies to all writing, but especially to writing that we want to be of use to children. Like it or not, the fact remains that most kids, and especially the thick, hairy ones, can't cope with obscenity out in the open. They're shocked in the most prudish way. So they shouldn't be: O.K. That's your problem, teach. . . .

The danger here is, that in trying to communicate something in their own terms in print, you will throw them by trying too hard. I'm not saying anything new: just that all that I've tried to get across is true (if it's true at all) in this area where both you and I operate.

We come back to the wider statement, that writing for children is no different from any other writing, except that it has to be better.

Quite a simple answer really . . .

And just the answer I would want to give myself. It is all a matter of finding writers who have the same sort of concerns that Alan Garner notes, and all the areas of concern I tried to list in an earlier chapter – as well as all the others left out. This is what one means by a writer for teenagers. His books will be read, as all good books are, by many others of other ages, but they seem to centre somehow on the teenager; especially if, like *The Owl Service*, they do as the *T.E.S.* says, 'present . . . a theme . . . to children no older than the characters in the story'. This is what we want and this is best of the ways we shall get it.

Yet it remains a fact that there is little opportunity and no encouragement to think in terms of producing literature like this. The solution to that problem is in other people's hands and so we had better look at it from their points of view.

PART THREE

Make Me An Offer

6

Portrait of a Supermarket

A LENDING library is, in a very accurate way, a supermarket – a help-yourself store. Books, like other goods, need to be shown, offered, advertised, sold. They need to be made attractive. Because they are material goods as well as works of art (some of them), they must come into competition with other material goods, as well as other media of expression and of entertainment. Every creative writer is an entertainer, a man in show business; besides all the other things he likes to believe he is. Few people feel they owe the creative writer a living, that he has a right to exist more than say a grocer or coal miner or a man who cleans the streets. Whether we, the bookish population, the professional bookfolk, believe the creative writer has an essential part to play in our daily lives or not, what *is* true is that the majority of the population, and every reluctant reader, has no such conception of the writer's place in society. In the eyes of the majority of the populace, he must work for his living and prove his worth before they will pay a penny to keep him alive, or expend a fingerful of energy to read his books. And it is no use our flying into a rage and using all sorts of high-flown language and ideas to prove anything else is the case. As we must teach from the known to the unknown, so in a consideration of reluctance we must work from what is so to what we would were so.

I have had the privilege of seeing a situation develop in which reluctant readers began to make a positive and lively response to books and reading, and in what follows in this chapter, I want to try and describe the ingredients that mainly contributed to that response, and to draw from these some conclusions as to the basic threads – the guide lines – which seem likely to be common factors in the stimulation of reading among reluctant readers.

In 1961 a secondary modern school of 500 + young people of both sexes aged between 11 + and 15 + settled into a new school building. The building contained a library room with space for 10,000 books, though at that time it

111

possessed about 2000, some in battered shape and few which a professional librarian would have regarded as being up-to-the-minute touchstones of present children's books of the best quality.

The architect's ineptitude had placed the room on the first floor of the building and made it an essential corridor via which to pass from one end of the building to the other. There are, in fact, five doors leading into the one room.

Through the work already done by a devoted English teacher it was established before the school moved to the new building, that, when settled, every form in the school should be in the library at least once during the week, and that most of the time allowed in this way was to be spent by the children in browsing, and borrowing books.

With shelves yawning, their new white wood showing brightly, the library routine began. Certain things were at once firmly stated:

1. The library was a separate place with its own rules and pupil staff who would run it and discipline it at all out-of-lesson times.
2. These pupil librarians were responsible to the teacher-librarian only: school prefects and other members of staff had only common rights within the place.
3. The work done in the library was to be carried out with as little compulsion as the member of staff concerned could bring himself to operate. Certainly, reading choice was to be as informally led and as uncompulsive as could be. And every class must regard as sacrosanct its weekly time in the library, and that time as primarily a borrowing and browsing time.
4. The rules were as few as possible, and though the discipline operated by the teacher-librarian was strict and formal at first, as soon as the routine and behaviour were established it became as relaxed and unobtrusive as could be managed.
5. It was early decided that the fiction shelves should grow as fast as possible, and it was while this was reviewed that the problem of 'right' books for such young people, most of whom were reluctant anyway by the time they reached the school, clarified itself.

For our purposes in this book, the first barrier and the first breakthrough came when the teacher of a backward class refused to bring her class to the library because she feared what her children might do to the books, and because 'There are so few books they would like anyway. There's nothing that's theirs.' No amount of talk could resolve the difficulty. Eventually the librarian hit upon the idea of throwing open an area of shelves on to which he promised to put anything, anything at all, which the backward classes brought in and gave him. Within a week he had over 200 copies of cheap annuals, Enid Blytons, and a smattering of the sort of peripheral works associated with these two commodities. Nothing daunted they were placed on the shelves and marked with a nasty and very large 'B' – not because, as was later thought, it meant Backward, but because it happened to be the only letter of the alphabet not used at that time in another part of the library. The section was, in fact, labelled 'Easy Readers'. The backward form swarmed in, hogged the corner, and began a process of devouring and demolishing *their* books. Within a year, that same form were searching the 'ordinary' fiction shelves (into which duplicate titles of some of the better Easy Readers had been slipped) and such was the surprise of the teacher that the other books they used were not eaten, torn, or scribbled upon more than would be expected anyway, that her two objections were soon exorcised.

Three years after the 'B' Readers were placed on the shelves, the tattered remains were burned. The job had been done. In the meantime, money had been found, books had been uncovered the 'backwards' would and could read, and they had begun to find other books, less obviously 'theirs' which they read as avidly.

But something else had happened, something less given to easy reporting. The attitude to books, the 'atmosphere' in which they were used and looked at, had changed, not only in that first experimental form, but in all the forms of 'backwards' who followed them, and who had never known of the 'B' Readers at all. Something carries over. Ask not how. It does. And this was a demonstration of it. Such a thing happened in another area of this experience of reluctant readers and books.

This was in the choice of books. After four years, the money allotted the library was increased 300 per cent by the enlightened authority under which the school is administered. The stock increased rapidly, and the choice of books and range of titles similarly. In the same period there came on to the market a number of useful writers and books for children of a reluctant nature: writers like E. W. Hildick, the Jet Books, Joan Tate, Josephine Kamm's two novels, *Fifteen*, and so on. The foundations were being laid. It soon became noticeable how these and similar books were chosen without any announcement of them by the teacher. They were nosed out, taken *before* any of the authors one would expect. At first this certainly had to do with the teacher-librarian who presented these books as skilfully as he knew how. But later, deliberately adopting a policy of no compulsion, even of this kind, deliberately attempting to find out what happened if these titles were left lying on the shelves, the pattern, this changed atmosphere, showed itself to be a self-sustaining thing. It was these same books which went out first. These became Five Star Books. They served to show that, within a situation of constant choice, a 'nose' for making choice develops. We all know this. It is part of the experience of the bookish as well as the reluctant: isn't it always difficult to sort out a book from the fiction shelves of a library one doesn't know well? Isn't a vast display daunting and constipating of choice? Too vast a collection is more frightening to a reluctant reader than no collection at all.

But at the same time it became an obvious truth within our specimen library that static stock, over-well-known stock, is also an encouragement to reluctance. After three years in a school, coming to the same library each week of one's school life, it is natural that, faced with the same 'mouldy' collection of 1000 fiction books, familiarity breeds, if not contempt, then certainly blindness: one sees only the titles one has read, is less and less willing to take from the shelves and make a real effort to read books one has not read, authors that are new. A changing stock, not a totally changing stock at every move, but a stock changed in part every so often, had an effect shown clearly in the daily records of books issued that were kept in this library for six years. Records not just of a general nature, but of the withdrawals of every child in the school on every occasion a book was borrowed, and indicating what 'kind' of book it was: even to the section within a section: that is, not just a fiction book, but a fiction book from the senior fiction shelves, or the County fiction shelves, etc.

Entirely by accident one other factor essential in the conversion of the reluctant reader at this secondary school age took control: the power of the group. It became the done thing at this school to read. In many forms there existed a clannish, group-conscious 'thing' about reading, particularly of certain titles. In the first year one of these titles was C. S. Lewis's *The Lion, The Witch and The Wardrobe*, and another was Townsend's *Gumble's Yard*. Everyone read them, most loved them, some hated them, some objected because most of the rest of the form found the books pleasurable. Whatever the reaction, it was one based on a group activity: the activity of reading a book at home in private and discussing it informally afterwards both in and out of a school classroom. Books had come alive, were a necessary and accepted part of daily life. And of corporate daily life.

This led to the next important stage in the work done by this one school library: its growth as a community bookshop. The teacher-librarian was faced with an apparently insoluble problem: in a school with a very high turn-over of borrowed books, a school in which most of the children attending read at least a book a week, the majority creative fiction, throughout four or five years; yet even so all the evidence pointed to a fall-off in reading activity when these same children left school. Far far too few of them took up the same activity as a public library borrower. Few bought books for themselves. One of the solutions, he believed, might lie in the creation of a book-buying public. There were other considerations. The children most likely to be responsive readers from their early days were usually those who came from homes in which books were visibly present in numbers, were seen to be read, and heard discussed. This is certainly not a panacea for the ills of the reluctant reader. Some children from very bookish homes are very un-bookish people, as Roe points out clearly in *Teachers, Librarians and Children*. Nevertheless, it is as sure as can be that if every home in the land possessed a small library of 200 or 300 well-chosen books, there would be many fewer re-luctant readers to cope with in the schools. For two sound reasons then it seemed a necessary part of the teacher-librarian's task to promote book possession as well as book borrowing. The details of such schemes as are useful are dealt with in the next chapter. It is only to be pointed out here that experience showed that the thinking was correct; buying books, possessing books, creates an attitude towards books which is helpful to the cure of reluctance.

In summary then, certain key-stones had been uncovered by the work of this school library which seem to me to be basic in the positive approach to the problem of the reluctant reader.

First, there must be as much opportunity as possible to come into contact with books, opportunity based on individual choice and taste, not on a pre-scribed list or a teacher's direction. This opportunity and choice must be exercised under an informal, unpernickety discipline which accepts that people will treat books with as variable respect as they treat their homes, their families and their possessions. The more books become part of accepted everyday life and as necessary as these other basics in living, the more will this be so.

Secondly, individual choice can only operate in a large but not overwhelming stock, and this in itself presents problems inherent in all 'stocked' goods, and the 'sale' of them.

Thirdly, the growth of the reading habit, like all habits, depends upon frequency, approbation by one's peers as well as one's elders. Once this corporate and individual attitude is established it snowballs into a self-sustaining activity. But like all habits it needs grooming, stimulation from time to time, and occasionally revitalising refreshment.

Fourthly, the problem is unlikely to be solved unless there accompanies the growth of the habit itself a permanent background of books possessed by the reader for his own. In the end, within our Western capitalist society, books follow the same cultural, social and economic patterns as other 'goods': where there is profit and possession there is also incentive and an increased activity.

These four threads have application in almost every professional book sphere: for teachers, librarians, booksellers and publishers. It is to a discussion of their individual response to the problem that I now come.

7

The Reluctant Teacher

THE section of the population who could do most – and who are doing most – about reluctance in reading are the teachers. Yet it is also true that they do most to create the problem.

The effectiveness of any teacher in the encouragement of the reading habit varies in proportion to the teacher's depth of knowledge of children's books and literature generally. So often is this remarkable that it seems almost a scientific law. The teacher who reads avidly himself, the teacher who knows and reads children's books, invariably fosters a similar interest in a high percentage of his pupils.

It seems almost inane to say so, but it is true that the teaching profession is a profession of reluctant readers. Many of them have no idea what children's fiction is like; almost as many never touch a work of fiction of any sort. They are seen to play games, drive motor-cars, garden, knit, smoke, do all sorts of other things their pupils imitate. They are rarely seen to read a novel, purr over it with pleasure, dwell on it with interest, talk about it with enthusiasm or anger; worse, they are never seen even carrying one. They are seen with chalky textbooks. They are heard hacking a set-book to pieces. But that is, the pupil says to himself, their job. The idea that it might be done for pleasure or out of any other necessity but that of making the money to buy bread and coal is not an impression one would gain from the behaviour of most teachers when they handle books. And it is of no use to storm at such criticism: it is the worm's eye view, and the worm turns back into the earth pretty smartly at the sight.

Let's trace the problem to the Colleges of Education. (They, of course, trace the problem back to the schools, for they are as frustrated by reluctance in their students as teachers are in their pupils.) Certainly in the last ten years the attitude to children's books in the colleges has changed: it has become more positive, more aware, more concerned. There are now a few colleges with advanced libraries, and growing children's libraries within them. There are a few men on the lecturing staffs who know children's books. But again: too few, too slowly, too often only after a battle, when a man with sufficient enthusiasm and stamina has built the library, effected the change in attitude by the sweat of his brow and perseverance. Fine, we say, they'll appreciate it all the more for that. But really! Is there any other trade, craft or profession which would tolerate, or be tolerated with such a slight knowledge of its basic tools? Would we put up with a surgeon who didn't know a scalpel from a bone saw, or a joiner who couldn't tell a claw hammer from a chisel? What would we have to say about a firm that didn't teach its apprentices how to manipulate their instruments, and what would we say about a young tradesman who didn't exercise himself in the use of them? Where in all the world is there a profession which throws its men out into practice without first showing them the tools of the trade? And all this is true of a number – the majority – of our colleges. Teachers are released into classrooms who have never seen a children's novel since they were children themselves: English students as well as History, Biology and Physical Education students. The problem is worse in the grammar schools, with their university-trained teachers. Amongst these last, and the academic mêlées they come from, children's books, and children's fiction especially, apart from the standard texts like *Alice*, have no standing at all. (It was interesting to notice recently the emergence among the student population at universities of a fashionable interest in *Pooh* and *Wind in the Willows* and *The Lord of the Rings* above all, and even in some of the later more academic children's writers like Rosemary Sutcliff. But it was almost an escapist interest, nothing to do with children's books as children's books.)

In some places there is even a situation in which the Education Authority is providing more money for children's libraries than the school staffs know how to spend. The teachers are just not available who know sufficient about school libraries and children's books to cope. For this very reason, students trained for School Library work by the one or two enlightened colleges which run rudimentary subsidiary courses of this nature are snapped up for posts of special responsibility immediately on graduation; and this is good neither for the students nor for the schools.

Until children's books and reading as an activity, not just as a process to be endured before the text is dissected, have gained some sort of standing, other than the fatuous lip-service at present paid them, things cannot improve.

Nowhere, in any college I know, are students told to go away and read, rather than listen to an hour's mundane talk. I have heard of one college in which the students were told to go away and spend the first term writing a novel. The lecturer had imagination and insight as well as courage. He had put his finger on one of the blatant weaknesses in our teaching methods throughout the educational spectrum: teaching staffs rarely do what they give their students to do.

How many teachers of the 'arts' subjects especially, engage in the 'exercises' they blandly set their pupils? In the first place many of us don't even read the books we recommend: school libraries are full of books the school librarian has never looked inside. We set exercises in writing poetry and stories for class work under the most fatuous working conditions, as any teacher who engages himself in the same activity will at once discover. We will expect a child to work creatively on quite different lines from an adult. But why should he? The child is a person as much as the adult: he is not a different form of being. His creative posture and methods vary quite as much and are as easily frustrated or inhibited. Sometimes one meets with teachers who have recognised the folly of such ways. An art teacher who talked to me recently told me of his surprise when he worked through a basic process in his art room which for years he had been expecting his children to perform, only to find that the process was extraordinarily difficult, and far too advanced for the children he usually gave it to. The exercise was a standard one recommended by his college for the children he taught. Not many teachers can be as honest with themselves and others as this. Fewer still remain fresh enough during their maturer years in the profession to think and respond so readily.

The point is that if we read more of the books we put on the shelves of our school libraries and recommend to our children we might find ourselves as surprised and moved to rethink our recommendations as was the teacher I quoted above to change his methods.

Such professional honesty leads one in the end to a position such as this which I quote from a letter by a grammar school teacher-librarian who is in fact more successful than he knows:

> All a school librarian can do for the 'reluctant reader' is, I believe, to put out an attractive display of well-chosen books and let the boys loose among them. I issue lists of recommended books, which are used a lot by boys in the first and second years; older boys ignore them. Because I am me and not you, they won't read a specific book I recommend or read out of. The intelligent ones of course will. The teacher-librarian can't do more, unless he is distinguished from THEM (authority) by being a Negro, like Braithwaite, for example, or unless he is more of a personality

than most of us, alas, are. To get more fiction read, I primarily need more money. The library is open throughout the school day (8.30–6.0) and most of the School come into it at some time, if only to read magazines. A more attractive selection of fiction to catch their eye would help most.

Though the tone of this sensitive and honest teacher, who works longer hours and harder than is fashionable, is one of near disillusionment, he has in fact put his finger several of the requirements for successful librarianship in a school.

First, what does not come out of his letter is that he knows his books. There are few novels that go into his library that he has not read. And this is the essential groundwork, which, along with his own personal enthusiasm for books and fiction especially, put some measure of success within his grasp.

Secondly, he has hit bottom which, in the end, we all reach: we must provide choice and opportunity to make it often.

Thirdly, he has found the essential limitations of his own ability to 'sell' books. There are no rules, no qualifications other than those stated already. Every teacher, out of his own reading experience and enthusiasms, will then find the methods that are successful *for him* in creating a reading interest in his pupils. The letter recognises the frustrating effect of 'authority', which in his case means that the pupils have been required to read certain set titles to a repellent extent. He recognises that most people are ordinary conscientious men and women with few extra special qualities to commend them, each with their own weaknesses and strengths. So much of what is written and taught in the colleges depends on the teacher having such an exceptional personality that he can carry off all sorts of otherwise impossible techniques.

So let us consider some of the techniques which depend not on the teacher's personality so much as his willingness to work. A number of points have already been covered in the previous chapter and these appertain here.

Ernest Roe, in the book I have often referred to already, criticises strongly the Library Lesson. At a one-day conference on The Library Market for Children's Books held on 2 June 1966 at the School of Librarianship North-Western Polytechnic, London, John Merrick, a teacher of some experience and a Principal Lecturer at Bulmershe College of Education, Reading, had this to say about this 'lessson' on the time-table:

'Library periods' during which pupils are instructed in the 'use of the Library' and 'Library assignments' which take little or no account of work actually going on in the classrooms are now seen to be largely irrelevant and perhaps actually harmful to the development of true, library-centred education. Instead of breaking down the barriers between subjects, which was their aim and *raison d'être*, such methods only too often reinforce them by suggesting that the library itself is just another subject. If this danger is to be avoided the library must somehow move into the classroom: not permanently, for that would prevent children from receiving the benefits to be derived from the presence of a balanced collection of books, but frequently enough for the books to really affect what goes on in the classrooms.

If Mr. Merrick means only what he says, I agree most heartily. Nothing is more artificial and contributory to reluctance than this harassed use of books, which is no more than another dose of words on paper such as is administered in every other subject in the school curriculum.

There has grown up, however, a heresy that needs burning out: that the library period as a separate entity is a nonsense; that there should be no time set aside in the time-table when classes are let loose in the library. This, of course, is to carry such criticism as Merrick's too far. Some time spent each week, when the child is allowed to handle books without reference to anyone or any 'subject' except by his own desire, is vitally important. Every child needs also to have the opportunity to borrow. We don't say that the dining-hall should never be entered but meals should be taken to the subject class-rooms and eaten there. We don't say that there is no need to provide time on the time-table for meals, for school doctors, for milk, for games, for learning instruments. Similarly those advocates of the library which is in theory always open but never allocated specifically find themselves defeated by the one weak link: humanity. By all means have the library open all the time, encourage staff to allow children to come to it at any time; but do not expect it to happen and the library to be used half as much as it will be if time is set aside on the time-table for each form, and those times expected to be used in the way I advocate. Headmasters too often prefer their corridors to be empty of boys and girls straying along to the library – it is at such times that so much 'crime' happens! Teachers prefer to teach their overcrowded classes as single units with little time for individual spur-of-the-moment absence in the library: things are neater done this way, more easy, more comfortable. We may not think this right or enlightened; we may chafe at the bit about it being so in many schools. But I am not interested in what ought to be so; I'm interested in what *is* so and how to legislate for the eternal humanity of man.

The library must always be open; but each form must have its allotted time in it. And in that time the important activity is that the child shall browse at will and borrow from as wide a choice as the teacher-librarian can afford.

And that he shall be helped in certain simple ways.

First, he must be helped to overcome his natural human laziness. Books need to be presented as tastefully as the librarian can manage, and as often as possible with their best side showing – usually the front of the dust cover.

Then a part of the fiction stock especially needs changing every so often – once a term say, but not much more often. This must be done and seen to be done, otherwise the boost a refreshed stock can give will pass unnoticed. One way of helping this mobility is to keep within the school's own stock a collection of books chosen and changed regularly by the local authority school library service. This has two distinct advantages. The first is that it is a section of the library which is regularly changed, with all the accompanying advantages as a stimulant. The second is that the library service stock will be selected by someone other than the resident teacher-librarian and will inevitably therefore reflect a different taste and choice. And this is often a needed counterbalance to a librarian who has strong preferences, which are bound to operate no matter how disinterestedly he tries to select for his library.

The teacher-librarian must constantly remind himself that the child's taste is to be respected. Only if he honestly does this will there be any dialogue between the teacher and the child which will allow of the teacher stretching the child into a more discriminating and enthusiastic reading habit than he already possesses. Comics provide an interesting extreme example here.

Many teachers go hot under the collar and red in the face at the very mention of comics, which they see as their arch enemy full of dreadful and crippling dangers to the pupils they are trying to educate. Such undisciplined reaction of such a violent nature makes them speechless about comics, and unable to react about them in any but a punitive or censorious way. Comics are barred, discussed only in dogmatic terms if at all, and when discovered, confiscated or publicly destroyed. Nothing is more likely to make the habit of reading comics an ingrained one.

The positive answer it would seem to me – apart from some gentle advice to the teacher himself to grow up and learn to contain his own prejudices and temper – would be to stock a set of *Tin-Tin, Hergé's Adventures of*, published by Methuen & Co. in translation from the original French. (And to stock alongside the relating French language editions.) *Tin-Tin* is comic strip, but comic strip as children will rarely meet it in 'comics'. The art work is of a fine quality, well executed and printed. The stories are long (each book contains only one). The comedy treatment is totally healthy and very humorous, and all the situations, though 'stock' ones, handled in an entertaining way. The balloons contain grammatically accurate language, the words making a credible story *on their own* besides being often necessary to an understanding of the tale and also far more numerous than in the usual comic. The colouring is subtle and balanced, and the picture arrangement varied and intelligent. There is no obvious attempt to moralise or teach, but Tin-Tin himself possesses the virtues of the traditional hero plus humour and the quality of being a figure of fun from time to time. All this is entirely healthy and laudable which makes a pity of the fact that *Tin-Tin* is bound poorly and so damages easily. A spell on *Tin-Tin* cannot help but make a child at least more aware of the deficiencies of his run-of-the-mill comic, if it does not wean him from comics entirely, and provides a point of contact between the teacher and the child for the discussion of comic material, for *Tin-Tin* is a product one can genuinely enjoy and like as an adult, while it offers quality material of 'comic' type with which to compare the shoddier stuff.

After a few months of trial and error, most alive young teachers know what their strengths are and what pitfalls to avoid in their ability to 'sell' books. The two basic things are knowledge, having read the books, and his own genuine enthusiasm for certain books. How this knowledge is presented, which books to present, is a matter for wide experimentation. The methods most generally used are:

> display in tasteful, economic ways;
> reading aloud passages from the book;
> recounting the story line;
> asking a child who has enjoyed it to recommend it to the class;
> presenting books linked by a theme, subject, character or by some other common denominator, not so much assessing the books or trying to stimulate interest in them, but merely using the children's own interests to spark off an interest in particular books because their story or whatever has to do with the children's own personal likes.

That the personality of the teacher and his own enthusiasms affect what his children read, and how each teacher develops his own techniques of sale are very clearly illustrated by the experience of Mr. Tom Wild, whom I have already referred to. This successful young teacher is a genuine enthusiast and possesses also a compelling personality very attractive to young people. His list of books he finds successful with reluctant secondary modern boys and girls is quite startling (by which I mean it is one I could never hope to use). Mr. Wild in a letter to me about it says this:

I rarely find a book 'sells' itself to reluctant readers. But I find I can sell the right book fairly easily.

1. Bill Naughton   — *Goalkeeper's Revenge* (boys and girls 3rd and 4th year).
2. Tolkien   — *The Hobbit* (with boys in the 2nd and 3rd years who happen to have missed it earlier on).
3. Wyn Griffith   — *The Adventures of Prydheri* (University of Wales).
4. Gillian Avery   — *The Warden's Niece* (goes like a bomb with the fourth form girls).
5. M. Baldwin   — *Grandad with Snails* (with first forms and seconds).
6. Laurie Lee   — *Cider with Rosie* (with 4th form girls).

I think that children have periods of reluctance when they genuinely cannot find a book to interest them. For them one has 'certs'. Certs? Nothing is all that certain with children and adolescents. But some books do seem to restore the desire to read which is temporarily lost:

7. Harper Lee   — *To Kill a Mocking Bird*.
8. Laurence Durrell *Bitter Lemons*.
9. Remarque   — *All Quiet on the Western Front*.
10. Steinbeck's shorter novels.
11. Some of the stories from Faulkner's *The Vanquished*.
(One boy has resisted my titles all year but read *1984*, one gets the impression very deeply, as he can talk fluent 'Newspeak' and the experience seems to have had a noticeable affect on him. The same boy is now 'hung' on C. S. Lewis's trilogy of SF books. At one time these were popular with a lot of the boys in class.)

By any standards there is some strong stuff here. I would guess some very esoteric stuff too, books not likely to be popular reading with many reluctant readers outside Tom Wild's influence. Or others like him. He gave a hint of how he does it:

> Esoteric? Yes. Deliberately so. 'This is something which is quite out of the ordinary especially for you.' I hand him/her the book, bestowing it like the white-man's burden on the Savage! The approach often works. It is the specialness of the occasion that does the trick. My girls will read Jane Austen if it is in my Folio Society edition!

The important thing is to find out what our successful methods are and to use them, not to copy slavishly other people's methods. When I see a list like Tom Wild's my first reaction is to think, my goodness what a strange collection! Books produce strong reactions. One must be careful not to think other people's 'odd' lists either better lists than one's own, or harmful lists. So long as they are based on a sound, discriminating reading, and not on ignorance and pot-luck, the child influenced by the recommendations will not be harmed. That the child himself comes to the books by other than critical routes matters not a jot. Tom Wild's delicious comment about Jane Austen makes just this point. I have, after all, met first-class rugger players who came to the game as boys because they liked rolling in mud.

Creating a book-buying population in school seems to me a natural extension of the work done in the school library. Architecturally it would be ideal if every school contained its own bookshop. There are two generally tried ways of selling books to children in school.

SCHOLASTIC PUBLICATIONS (64 Bury Walk, London S.W.3). This is an educational distributive firm. Twice each term they send to member schools mail order sheets, listing and illustrating the eighteen choices of titles available on each occasion. There is a newsletter for each pupil and an information sheet for the teacher: both are useful, the one as a stimulant, the other as an aid to the teacher who wants to guide his children's reading. The firm operates a list directed at each educational age level and offers a number of advantages as a means of bringing children to book-buying.

This happens only twice a term. The 'rhythm' is important. It is neither too often nor too rare. The book agencies I discuss below find that interest tends to fall off considerably after a time: because it is always 'there', the book shop can fade into the landscape and be forgotten.

The list is a sufficiently small one in number of books offered not to frighten the child away by its bulk (to the reluctant outsider looking in, bookshops always seem to be a maze of indigestible books). And yet there are sufficient titles for most children to find one book out of the eighteen which attracts him.

The books are selected by a team of people, most of whom are teachers, and whose primary interest in the firm is not financial. Therefore the titles selected, one can be sure, have gone through the mill of discussion and consideration which I earlier suggested was an important factor in any selection and recommendation. I have been present at some of Scholastic's selection meetings and been enormously impressed not only by the genuine concern of every one in the firm to do the best he can by the children, but also by the amount of energy and time devoted to the selection of the books they offer.

Scholastic's problem, as for us all, is to find sufficient paperback titles of books that meet their standards and needs. This is particularly true at the SCOOP CLUB stage – that for the secondary school – when they are faced with the difficulties which occupy us in this book.

A further distinct advantage of S.P. is the simplicity of the money changing. It would take unavailable space to go into all this here, but certainly it is a point to be made, that the responsibility for stock and money involved in an agency makes this method of doing the job very much more bothersome.

Scholastic Publications' methods are reasonably easy, safe and unburden-some.

THE BOOK AGENCY itself is really a branch of a local bookshop based in a school. In theory and under certain conditions in practice, it is the fullest answer to the problem. Many teachers' experience has shown, however, that if handled wrongly, the agency is a failure after the first few weeks of busy-ness, and certainly a headache to the teacher involved.

The required conditions would seem to me to be:

1. That a good professional bookshop is responsible for the agency, preferably staffs it, and certainly controls the stock insofar as the processing is concerned.
2. That there exists between the responsible teacher and the bookseller a sympathetic agreement about what is meant to be achieved by a school bookshop. This will probably mean that the stock is selected by the teacher and the bookseller in conference; that opening times, any possible financial or other concessions, and 'booster' occasions are similarly dealt with.
3. That the bookseller understands that it may take time before the agency is a profit-making business; that there will certainly be a fall-off in business after the first flush, and that to keep the agency a successful one will require what I have called 'booster' occasions: that is, book fairs, or weeks; specially aimed and timed events which will create that first fine careless rapture. Unless the bookseller is prepared to co-operate in all these the teacher is hanging round his neck a millstone he may regret.
4. It is only by such agreement between the teacher and the bookseller that the continuity which makes an agency a vital part of the school landscape can be achieved, for otherwise all is dependent on the energy and stamina of the one responsible member of staff who might in any case move jobs at some time in the future.
5. Finally, without storage room, which can be locked, and presentation space which is an effective point of sale within the school, little can be achieved and much can be lost.

Booksellers are waking up to the fact that in a school is a potential custom of sizable and financially lucrative proportions, and that captive here is their future custom, waiting to be introduced to them and their trade. The appearance on the market of so many more children's paperback series has helped their response and about these very variable products I have things to say in Chapter 9.

As I see it, then, the library within a school is a centre which allows for as much opportunity as possible and far more than I have met in any school within my own experience, for children to come into an informal, individual contact with books; a place in which their own tastes and needs can run riot among the stock which has itself been catholically selected by the teacher-librarian; a place where books may be looked at, borrowed and bought, and from which they will undoubtedly be stolen if the library is a successful one.

Its work does not end there, and the work is not the sole prerogative of the teachers responsible for organising and using the library directly. It extends, as Mr. Merrick pointed out, into every other room in the school. Most importantly it can do this by setting up, as soon as money and stock will allow, class libraries which contain standard reference books, books of particular use to that room or teacher or class, and at least 100 carefully selected fiction books. These decentralised libraries bring books into the life of every child in the school, every school day, not by requirement or control, but merely as they would do in any well-established home: by being around, by the fact that they are 'there', as chairs are there and tables, crockery and all the other civilised needs of mankind. We must somehow achieve a balance between the oblivion of familiarity, and the frightening awe created by things 'not for us, but only for "them" '. The point of balance comes when the books are there in sufficiently large quantities to be noticeable (a 'few' in a cupboard don't qualify), when the stock contains attractive things which will suit the tastes and needs of their audience (it's no good putting E. M. Forster in the backward class, but there should be, for example, some Joan Tate books in most middle school forms), and when the familiarity is spring-cleaned by an active teacher who renews the stock occasionally. Reluctance is an attitude more often than an inability, and so we must seek to re-educate the attitude, and provide the circumstances which prevent its growth.

Given space, I would want to say much about the more directed use of books during English (and other subject) lessons, about set-books, about our methods of 'study' and 'criticism', about the titles we choose for such work, and the 'exercises' we give to consolidate the work. To begin on such topics invites me to doom, however, and I must leave such morsels alone, suggesting that David Holbrook's *English for Maturity* is still the most considered and stimulating work which includes some of these things, even though one disagrees with much that Holbrook says. I have not been able to resist the temptation to suggest titles for classroom 'work' in the lists in Part Four.

Perhaps I should end this chapter by singing again the praise of creative writing as an art form of *entertainment*, for herein lies its first cause; that, as E. M. Forster says with tongue in cheek about the novel, 'Yes – oh dear – yes – the novel tells a story'. If there are writers for adults who would nowadays deny that it need to, young people's writers, and teachers do so at their peril. Let us not despise that laudable intention, nor sully it by supposing that good creative writing must be 'taught' by tearing it to pieces; and let us not insult an author who has sweated some weeks, months and sometimes years over his work by thinking that our job as teachers is to interpret him by endless dull talk after one brief reading – if that – of his book. Primarily let us not suppose that if we have selected well we must continue the imposition of ourselves and our tastes upon other people – the children we teach – by insisting they select our selection from the selection we have already made.

8

The Reluctant Librarian

LIBRARIANS are reluctant about books in quite a different way from most other mortals. They are often very well-read people: it is among the children's public librarians one finds the most informed knowledge of children's books. I doubt not that they are conscientious, professional people: they care for books (too much, often); they care for the people who use them (no librarian anywhere has ever been rude to me or too busy to help me, and they have put up with my overdue behaviour without ill temper for many years); while among the Schools Service librarians there are some of the most militant workers in the cause of reading and books that I have met. Their private machinations make my own grumbles sound like the cheepings of an impatient fledgling.

The reluctance of far too many librarians lies in their refusal to move out with any energetic zeal into the world at large and encourage people to come in. They sometimes seem satisfied with the 40 per cent, and oblivious to the very existence of the non-reading, submerged 60 per cent. On the other hand, the public library possesses a number of the requirements for success with the reluctant reader: opportunity, informality, self-directed choice, breadth and size of stock. On the other hand, it presents ingrained disadvantages. Each of these I must dwell on.

The hush-barrier. The rubber-soled silence. Yes, quietness is a need. Yes, one must remember there is 40 per cent of the population who seem to like libraries and need them, and who cannot be denied in order to catch the others. Yes, the public library must cater for old as well as young, intellectual as well as cerebrally thoughtless. But there are too many biblio-buildings, places where books come first and people second, silence before the noise of popularity, poker-faced placidity before explosions of delight. Books must be stared at through a Greek tragic mask – or so it seems if one observes for a

129

(quietly) hilarious morning the behaviour of most library users. All this makes it difficult to contain elbow-wide, free-voiced adolescents. But let's come to the concrete.

Forbidding is a word that says a lot about why public libraries are not used by reluctant readers, even supposing they ever pass the doors. The answer to that is an architectural and decorative one. Things are improving, as new libraries are built.

Inside – after the hush-barrier has been broken – the problem is one of what to look at, where to go; just as it was a problem to the backward class I referred to in Chapter 6. They wouldn't be able to find 'anything which is "theirs" '. In a public library, the reluctant reader is a backward child. Undoubtedly he will recognise two things as 'his':

> the popular magazines,
> and paperbacks.

In these two products of the popular press, the reluctant teenager finds a natural ally and a known way. Where are they in the public library? In most, the answer is, they aren't. The popular magazines, if taken at all, are half-hidden in the smaller libraries, and put in a separate room in the larger places.

Paperbacks can turn some librarians red of face and grey of hair at their mention as suitable, desirable things to stock in libraries. Yet, Lorna V. Paulin, President of the Library Association, in her address to the School Library Association Annual Conference on 30 December 1966, said this:

> What should the public library do to encourage young people to use its service? Apart from obvious measures which apply to readers of all ages, such as making the library a friendly, welcoming place, providing a good stock of books in comfortable and convenient surroundings, arranging a variety of book displays, and generally providing as good a service as possible, there are some things that can be done specifically with young people in mind. The libraries must realise, to begin with, that they are appealing to many different kinds of young people – or to the same people in different moods and at different times which comes to the same thing – and remember to cater for a wide range of interests and of enthusiasm for reading.

All this many a run-of-the-mill librarian might have said. But the President went on in words only too few would have used:

> It is here that paperbacks come into their own. I used to be doubtful of the wisdom of providing paperbacks in public libraries, but I am not now, as I have seen what an enormous difference a good display of paperbacks makes to whether young people use the public library or not. It appears that many a teenager, entering a library and seeing nothing but thousands (literally thousands) of hardbacked books

on all sides, decides, however colourful these books may be in their plastic jackets, that the library is not for him. A collection of paperbacks, however, preferably near the entrance of the library and arranged so that their covers and not only their spines are displayed, is very likely to prove attractive. In Hertfordshire we have made a special feature of such displays in Hitchin and Stevenage libraries, and they have been almost embarrassingly successful. (*The School Librarian*, Vol. 15, Number 1, p. 27.)

In other words: work from the known to the unknown. From the accepted to the rejected. From the familiar to the formidable. From the soft edge of literature to the hard edge of bibliomania. We never know – there might even come a time when those paperbacks can be moved from prominence by the door, to an obscure shelf, and from obscurity at last to the dustbin, just as those annuals and cheap pulp books in the Easy Readers section were at the school I spoke of in Chapter 6.

Paperback stocks are but a beginning. Sheila Ray, one of the most alive Children's and Youth Librarians, when working in Leicestershire, wrote this to me:

> Teachers are, I think, in the best position to do something about the submerged 60 per cent. Librarians, I think, must make an all-out effort with the under-11's. After this it is difficult to get young people into the libraries unless they are already sold on the idea. I think libraries could be made into much more attractive places. In Sweden I have seen libraries absolutely over-run with teenagers – they had coffee bars, teenage rooms and were really inviting! One even had a bookshop – and I'm sure this is a valid idea especially in communities such as large villages or small towns, where a 'full-time' bookshop isn't an economic proposition.

Mrs. Ray brings out some important ideas. First, she is probably right in supposing that the public libraries can best encourage the reading habit with younger children. With the growth of children's libraries as a separate room or even building, this is a possible and rewarding task. But it still remains true that a large number of those younger children will drop the library habit at teenage, merely because the atmosphere of the adult public library is alien to the teenage way of life, and it is of no use our bemoaning this, or ignoring it: it is a permanent fact of social behaviour and must be accounted for if we really want to retain the majority of people as avid, developing readers.

So the Swedes are right. Rather than ignore the problem, take the bull by the horns: set up libraries for these 'middle years', this present 'no-man's land', and make something of what these years are: extreme, searching, group-dominated, self-conscious, and socially almost ethnic. One of the librarians' problems, often discussed, is where to put books suitable for teenage, and with more and more being published the problem becomes more and more acute. They shouldn't be in the children's library; they are lost in the adult library. Most librarians seem to favour a separate section within the adult library. But that is to frustrate the ideal. Such a context is unattractive to a teenager, who gains his strength because lots of others do it; because he can feel a distinct apartness, a visible dissociation from adults, and because the teenager today expresses himself in modes, manners and rituals vastly different from and even alien to and misunderstood by 'respectable', 'old-fashioned' adults. Again I take no stand: I merely postulate what is so and seek to legislate for it. This situation is not going to change soon, and we may as well recognise it and contain ourselves in patience if not in faith. Provide an atmosphere in which books and teenagers are brought together under the hand of a sympathetic librarian who knows his stock and his teenagers, and the result will be what Sheila Ray saw: a place 'absolutely over-run with teenagers'. Reading teenagers.

Just as the natural, proper extension of the school library is the creation not just of a reading public but a book-buying public, so is this true of the public library. Book-selling in this country is in a shabby state. There are hundreds of towns without a shop that can be called a *book*shop, and hundreds of smaller communities without contact with anything approaching even a newspaper shop. Every one of these towns and communities has its full-time or part-time library, or its travelling library van at the very least. The book-sellers complain rightly that the manpower of sufficient intelligence and knowledge to deal professionally with books is in remarkably short supply. Every library contains just such people: trained, knowledgeable, intelligent. As a means of bringing people who would otherwise stay out into the libraries, as a service to the community which can only benefit both the libraries and the community, bookselling is a valid task for the public librarian. Yet even as I write that sentence I know I carry very very few of the librarians with me.

One can understand their objections. One can analyse their reactions: professionalism offended (we still feel librarianship is cultural and bookselling merely 'trade'); rivalries provoked (libraries and bookshops are still thought to be in opposition, as though book borrowers diminish the potential number of book buyers and vice versa); understaffed, overworked libraries quoted (rightly); a wrong emphasis on library function argued (libraries are said to be store houses of information and the staffs their guardians and servants). Against all this, whether right or wrong, is one solid, undeniable fact: in a 'literate' country the great majority of the population never truly engage in the most civilising activity of civilised society. None of us who recognise this, and have the cure within our grasp can abdicate from responsibility for the state of things, or from remedial activity.

To continue the suggestions: as a public service the public libraries have the power to reach out into every home in the land. Without taint of commercialism, or fear of any antagonism but that of bigotry, they can publicise books, encourage, stimulate, suggest – generally engender an attitude of mind which accepts books and reading as important to daily life. Some librarians already do all they can to produce lists, especially at Christmas time, which might help parents in the choice of books for their children; they promote holiday competitions; turn out duplicated magazines freely distributed. But the entire strategy is far too piece-meal, too erratic, too thin on the ground to have much of an effect except in pockets and strongholds held by enthusiastic, dedicated people. A once-a-year National Book Week is not enough. This is something that should not need spot-lighting, because it should be something integral and central to daily life throughout the land.

9

The Reluctant Publisher

THE problem of publishing for teenage young people arises almost entirely because the publishers have never decided that there is such a market as the teenage market; do not accept that there is any editorial requirement for a separate entity from the children's department. Almost alone among the producers of mass media, the book publishers have not kept up with nor track of the growth in teenage social behaviour and needs. Next door to them the disc men, Carnaby Street, TV and radio, the popular magazine and paper press, and even the film makers have not only come to terms with the phenomenon but taken the initiative, so that what was once a genuine up-surge from the street-corner days of teenage life has now become a com-mercially directed, adult-engineered, socially independent group: The Teenagers.

The signs are that there is an awakening among the book publishers. But in what a fashion it comes! First of all, the other commercial concerns recog-nised at once that teenagers do not regard themselves as 'children', nor do they want to ally themselves with adults: they want their own, highly charac-teristic mode. Pop culture men fastened on to this early, and now stimulate these attitudes ruthlessly in the promotion of their trade, to the extent that it is now immaterial whether what we see continues to be the genuine reflec-tion of young people's thinking and imagination or the interpretation of it by the ad. men. What the publishers ought to have learned and haven't is that this gives a clear indication that book publishing for teenagers needs a separate editorial department, certainly *not* connected in the public mind with children's publishing; and preferably not contained within adult departments. Just as the children's departments had to be created years ago, so now we must create teenage departments. Their books need separate promotion, and distinct production design, that attract the market they are aimed to supply.

In my view, it is only by doing this will publishers achieve some success with the reluctant readership of most of the teenage population, the time of life when the problem becomes ingrained; and will reach with any real financial success the young people's market which at present is only touched in a small way. But to do this with integrity and responsibility other factors need to be considered.

The most important aspect of the answer to the problem must be the methods by which the books themselves are found. Children's and educational publishers, who so far have handled the 'older children's' books, have worked for years with a majority of authors whom they treat very much as scribes: the writers turn in a book which the editors then work at, until together, with paste and scissors in some cases, the editor and the authors 'write' the books. This is not to say there are no genuine, professional, even brilliant writers among the children's authors. There are. But few, and too many who are hacks of the paste-and-scissors type. And too many editors who see such editorial practice as their function. If we are to achieve young people's books of quality and real worth then both this attitude to their production and the rate of payment of the authors must be revised.

Hack writers, as Jay Williams suggested in his comments about the American situation, tend to work fast, for what they can come by. Genuine authors tend to work much more slowly and even have to live off what they earn. (There are publishers who seem to feel it is something of a crime for children's authors to expect to live off their royalties.) Apart from this, the authors we would want to write for this market are often also capable of earning very much more in other spheres of work than they can from the present children's writers' terms. I would average the amount at two-thirds more than can be earned writing for the young.

The publisher's answer is likely to take the line that the royalties offered the children's writers is based on a very real assessment of what children's books cost to produce and what they bring in from sales. Antony Kamm, Editor in Chief of Brockhampton Press, in an article in *The Author* for Autumn 1967, gave a set of figures to show how this operates. No one doubts Mr. Kamm's figures. He is one of the children's publishers who knows what he is about. What I would want to say is that so long as the publishers allow the situation to remain as it is in the promotion and sale of children's books then these same figures will operate and the wheel will always come full circle. Somewhere it must be broken. Someone must make the break. The author can't: if he writes a truthful young people's book, it will too often be rejected by the publishers, or considerably savaged in the editorial department before it sees the light of day. So the books aren't written. The book-seller, librarian and teacher can't make the break, because the books aren't there to promote. And the young people can't make the break because they must first be stimulated to buy (or borrow) the books which then have to be 'right' if they are to go on buying (or borrowing) and make the business of producing the books profitable.

Only the publisher, with his capital and most of the other reins in his hand, can possibly bring about the redirection that is needed and which it is almost too late to make.

Some have begun. But they have begun in such a way that one trembles for the outcome: either their presuppositions are profoundly in error, or their actual productions are of such a quality that one would prefer they did not put the books on the market. Or both.

The presuppositions first.

Vaguely aware that there is gold in them there pockets, various publishers have attempted to cash in on the market by turning out children's books in paperback, marketing them through newsagents and general stores as well as through the bookshops (which on the whole are not frequented by the majority of children). The age range of almost all these attempts is usually stated as 8–15, some of them also attempting in various ways to group the books for ages within the series.

Puffin Books had been going years before anyone seriously tackled the children's market. These are still the best turned out, best selected set of books for children available.

The explosion in children's paperbacks during the last five years has had amazing success. First of all Armada Books, now part of Collins, turned out reprint titles of popular adventure stories. Dragon Books, now part of Granada, had alarming success: they sold over a million copies in the first three months of publication. Their success was alarming because, in my far from infallible view, these books were the worst-selected, poorest-produced books of all the 'respectable' children's paperbacks. They epitomise for me what happens un-necessarily in mass-produced publishing unless great care is taken to resist the temptations. Such a statement needs some explanation, and I would be doing Dragon Books an injury not to do so, for I don't believe they are entirely motivated by purely commercial interests.

The first range of Dragons included: *Beau Geste*, *My Friend Flicka* in two parts, and *Coral Island* 'retold'. Of these, *Beau Geste* struck one as an unlikely winner: but it was timed to appear as a film tie-in. Result: it reprinted. *My*

Friend Flicka (as a horse story, a natural commercial winner) was published in a two-volume effort. No doubt production costs required it if Dragons were to keep the price at 2*s*. 6*d*. a copy. *Coral Island* was the saddest of the batch. The rewrite was clumsy, the first eight pages of the original being contained in the first two of the Dragon version, and with very few of the original sentences left undiluted. The fact that it was rewritten was not stated on the front cover, but mentioned only in the back cover blurb and on the half-title page inside.

Dragon's covers are, like the first Armadas, lurid, cheap in the quality of art-work and production, and the paper and typography coarse. They were sold with a stimulant: a competition intended to generate a chain reaction in Dragon's market, by encouraging the participants to introduce another child to the books, and offering prizes of a variety of goods very attractive to children: cameras, bicycles, transistors, and even a pony.

Even if one could accept – and I cannot – that these books are turned out from the purest of motives and concerned thinking about children and reading, they remain the saddest, most unfortunate products of the 'respectable' publishing industry for years. There is no need to debase quality and even to defile original texts in order to get children to buy and read. To think so is a fallacy, born of inexperience with children and books, or out-and-out commercialism of the worst kind. Anyone in close touch with children on a daily basis knows that a good-quality text, in a good-quality production will be bought and read if the price is right (not more than 3*s*. 6*d*. at present) and the book is right (as I've tried to show) and the cover is right (and about this we must say some things). One can have some confirmation of this even as things are at present. Knight Books, the paperback division of Brockhampton Press, has been producing for a year (at the time of writing) and has already established itself as one of the best children's paperback series. Knight Books are produced with enormous care and attention. Their titles include a very wide range of standard – from Blyton and Biggles to *The Boy Who Was Afraid* – but their production quality is levelly high throughout. They, like Dragon Books, have attempted a grading system for age, and with the Hodder paperback operation to market them, have found their way into a goodly number of outlets. Without any extra stimulus to support them, all the indications are that Knights are doing extraordinarily well. And they deserve to. One big wholesale firm, in fact, wrote this to me: 'Our best sellers (through the newsagent outlets) are the Knight Books. These are the best series in paperback and therefore we now handle only these.'

It is my opinion that no production or selection need fall below that set by Knights.

The second presupposition, which even Knight Books has made, is that the teenage, reluctant market can be tackled by building up to it from the safe and tried children's market. Thus Knights, Dragons, and Peacock Books themselves (the follow-up to Puffins, again on the market before anyone else tackled the teenager) all state their age range as ending at 15. One gets the feeling that each one of these new series hopes eventually, when they are established, to push that age up to 17 or 18. But even as they stand there is a basic error of judgement. Children begin to look about for what they consider teenage things at about 11 and 12. By 13 this attitude is deep seated. Things which then smack of childhood are rejected. Thus books which are allied to children's books begin at a disadvantage. There is no such market for a book as the 8–15-year-old.

Peacocks failed commercially, as one guesses they did, because they presented the wrong books to the wrong market: bookish children, which Peacocks supplied, have left children's books and gone without much effort to adult books. The unbookish would not accept Peacocks because the selection was wrong and the presentation that of children's books rather than adolescent books. With, of course, one or two interesting exceptions, especially *Fifteen*, Peacocks' most successful title.

Knights will not do so well as they might at the older end of their range because the books they present tend to be long and are allied to Knights Paperbacks for Children.

What is necessary, as I have stated before, is a series dissociated altogether from children's and adult books and which makes a straight appeal to the adolescent population. And this appeal need not be made on any catch title, like Teenager or Adolescent, or Young People's books. It can be done purely on the method of presentation and the selection of the books.

We can learn here from the young people's magazines. They now hardly need to state their appeal. Their 'look' – the cover, the blurb, the selection of items to write up – make that statement for them. Look at the titles:

Rave, Petticoat/Trend, Honey, Disc.

These are words which speak their age and appeal without ever mentioning age or level. Their cover pictures: full colour, featuring people of the age to which the magazine is directed, again state the appeal. I am not advocating that this is precisely what the book producers should do in exactly similar artistic terms. I am saying that age and appeal can be suggested without direct statement; and that this is more important than statement. It is after all true that publishers state an age for the children's books they produce, and often this stated age is years wrong when one looks at the children who actually read the books. Often this is the result of the packaging: the cover or the title or both suggest a younger or older age than the publisher intended. Art-work is particularly prone to this, and art-work is the common technique used for children's and older children's cover designs.

As we discovered earlier in this book, adolescence is a time when the appealing quality is that of realism: realism in the sense that colour photographs seem to be more effective than full-colour art-work; that in art-work itself realism, or at least the current interpretation of it at any particular time, is preferred to any other. Brightness, colour, direct, bold statement in art-work, and a concern for teenage people* rather than any other age seem to be the required elements in appealing presentation for adolescents.

Once again *Fifteen* by Beverly Cleary, when it was first published here by Peacock Books, carried a cover photograph of a young girl looking straight at the camera. Teenagers found that face irresistible – it was exactly what was needed by way of cover presentation. When one compares this book with others in Peacock my point becomes fairly obvious, I think.

Given a series of paperbacks unattached and unassociated with any children's series, written with the themes, subjects and treatments in mind, such as we have already discussed, one would have the basis of a literature that *would* supply the reluctant adolescent with fiction he finds compelling. Not all the books, all the time: but some of them most of the time. And this would be an advance worth making: worth making educationally, and commercially.

Another presupposition concerns the books either chosen or commissioned for the adolescent market. Either suitable adult books are reprinted, as in Peacocks, or, more often than not, a children's author attempts to do a book for this older range. There are dangers in both directions.

The adult books tend to be second rate, competent novels, mostly published five years or more before they are brought out for the teenager. Their feel is that of a 5-year-old book, an adult book that will 'do', a cast-off, as father's clothes used to be given to the gangling teenage son. Now that just

* Bear in mind that 'teenage' is officially considered in commercial circles, and it would seem among the young people themselves, to begin at 13 and to end at 21.

will not do. There *are* occasionally adult books one would want to have for young people: *Old Mali and the Boy* by D. R. Sherman is a case in point, Steinbeck's short novels are others. But generally speaking this is a second rate way of doing the job.

As for the children's authors! If they are 'names' then they are already associated with children's books, read earlier. More affecting is the difficulty established children's authors seem to have in breaking out of the thought forms, the verbal restrictions, the plot patterns of children's books. Some authors have tried, with varying success, but none, except Garner, with any total success, it seems to me. Dorothy Clewes is an example. She has written a number of competent children's books, and in 1967 published from Collins an attempt at a teenage story, called *A Boy Like Walt*. True the book is *about* teenagers, but it is not *for* teenagers, even though that is what Miss Clewes intended. It will be read with enjoyment by 10–12-year-olds as a story about boys older than themselves. As a story right for people the age of those in the story, it fails. Miss Clewes either has not broken away from the children's book, or she has not fully understood the needs and thought forms of the adolescent. Neither does her publisher, who jacketed the book in a cover that is children's not teenage in appeal.

Malcolm Saville did the same switch with his Simon Baines thrillers which William Heinemann publish. Saville was more astute about the things which appeal to the adolescent, and tells entertaining stories. With my own youngsters they have succeeded, but I feel they have done so more with those who first of all found his Lone Pine books, and wanted more Saville. They did not stand up in their own right. Saville, in fact, has been limited by his own prolificity as a children's author, and by the fact that his books for young people were published and sold by a children's department. And it is this last fence – the children's department – which is most likely to bring to failure any of us who attempt to write for teenagers.

Publishers have a neurosis about having a 'name' on their lists. It is interesting to see how limited in their sources is every one of the new children's paperback products: Blyton, Johns, Buckeridge, Saville, occur with monotonous frequency; followed by the other second-flight pops: the Sue Barton books, William, even Bunter, and the like. There has been little of adventure in finding new authors for children, let alone adolescents. And in publishing for adolescents 'names' are difficult to find, for there are few true writers for adolescents. When the publishers are prepared to venture, and prepared to venture with real willingness to pay for good books, then the authors will come to light who *can* do this. They will be found in two places: among the adult authors who have a feeling for young people and the right qualities in their writing; and among the very young writers who often at present seem to begin their careers on the magazines.

I feel this last to be the most fruitful hunting ground. Anyone who really knows the young of today – knows them at first hand and by experience – cannot be older than 25 to 30, for this is the first generation which has come through: which has experienced at first hand the contemporary teenage phenomenon. They only have that instinctive feeling for the language, the themes, the treatments which communicate with present-day young people. But because they are the 'new generation' they will not put up with the kind of limitations and savagery of children's departments in handling their work. They will want a freedom the children's departments will not, or cannot allow. 'We can't put that out when it might be read by children of 8 or 9', say they. True: which is yet one more reason for the Teenage Department. Until there is a separate publishing department which makes it clear to everyone in the professional book business that these books are meant for adolescents, will be all right for adults but not for children to read, then there is no real hope that we can achieve the artistic freedom needed.

Consideration of the promotion of books for any age, let alone teenage, leaves one feeling strongly the inadequacy of British publishers to make their products so part of everyday living that they are successfully marketed. There is little by way of newspaper advertising except in the 'quality' journals; there is nothing at all on TV or radio; one sees no hoarding or public display advertising outside London. The problem, say the publishers, is that there are so many books, each an individual item on the book market, as opposed to a trade name for a soap, which remains the same from month to month, year to year. And even accepting this as a valid argument, one still needs to ask why it is that books as books, reading as an activity have never been collectively promoted by the book-making businessmen. That at least would bring to people's attention books as products and reading as an activity. There is 'something not quite nice' about advertising like this, something degrading to books and 'quality' book production. Indeed? That's an odd sort of ostrich attitude that any businessman in his senses in a capitalist, advertisement-ridden society scorns at his peril. There is an odder touch of incest about the publishing industry's promotion. Show cards for bookshops; adverts in the trade journals; these follow debased techniques similar to the rest of the general advertising industry: sex, appeals to human foible, verbal *double entendre*, all the candy floss of the ad. man. They are, it seems, primarily intended to be seen by those who sell books. The adverts rarely spill into the outside world. It is remarkable that they are considered correct or at least allowable within the enclosure of book circles, but not in competition with other kinds of goods outside those circles. The publishers have failed utterly to present a united book-promotional front to society at large, but hang for grim death on to film and TV rights, and link-ups with such other money-spinners as they can muster. Books are always secondary to something else, as in 'the book of the film'. There is no frontal attack firmly stating the merits of books themselves, and the value and pleasure of reading as a form of financial outlay. Books remain therefore for most people a fringe activity, a free lending library provision should one feel moved to use it. 'You don't want another book, dear – you've got one at home' is a hoary trade joke: and as we laugh, as we always do, let's remember that it is also in part an indictment of the failure of our promotion of book possession.

In the face of all this, one realises, one is crying for the moon to suggest that there ought to be book-promotion adverts in the teenage magazines – including the special interest mags. – on TV and the commercial Pop radio. We have given in to the idea that the majority of people *won't* read, and cling on to the hope that we can all discover the one book in a thousand that will make our little pile. Every writer, every publisher, wants a best seller, and so we develop the formulas, debased and mechanically produced, which have in the past secured best sellers. We proclaim the successors to Bond, to Braine, to Sillitoe and Sagan. With few if any names to conjure with, it is not surprising that the teenage market is fought shy of by publishers: those reluctant entrepreneurs. This is, they say, a market to be opened up, to be discovered, to be experimented in: untried, uncertain, probably lucrative – but let's tread warily, and wouldn't it be better if someone else trod the path first?

PART FOUR

Appendixes

Appendix A
Five Star Books

THESE titles have been found by a number of teachers, librarians and book-sellers to excite an immediate response from young people who otherwise find creative fiction dull and unattractive. All seem to me to satisfy a sufficient standard of quality in their writing.

The books range in age, appeal, and difficulty over the intelligence and age spectrum considered in this book. No attempt has been made to indicate any of this in relation to each title because such indications are too often misleading. Ideally, the books should be available to all the children involved, who will select most wisely for themselves.

Author	Title	Publisher
Buchan, John	The Thirty-nine Steps	Dent, and Pan
Chambers, Aidan	Cycle Smash	Heinemann Pyramid
	Marle	Books
Cleary, Beverly	Fifteen	Peacock Books
Doyle, Conan	The Adventures of Sherlock Holmes	John Murray
Garner, Alan	Elidor	Collins, and Puffin Books
	The Owl Service	Collins
Golding, William	Lord of the Flies	Faber
Hildick, E. W.	Birdy Jones	Faber, and
	Louie's Lot	Pan-Macmillan TOPLINERS
	Louie's S.O.S.	Pan-Macmillan
	Birdy and the Group	TOPLINERS
Huxley, Aldous	Brave New World	Chatto & Windus, and Penguin Books
Innes, Hammond	Campbell's Kingdom	Collins
Jerome, Jerome K.	Three Men in a Boat	Dent
Kamm, Josephine	Young Mother	Brockhampton Press
	Out of Step	and Heinemann Educational Books (N.W.S.)

Author	Title	Publisher
Lewis, C. S.	*The Lion, the Witch and the Wardrobe* And the other volumes in the *Narnia Saga*	Bles, and Puffin
Maddock, Reginald	*The Pit*	Collins
Naughton, Bill	*Goalkeeper's Revenge*	Harrap
Schaefer, Jack	*Shane*	Deutsch
Shute, Nevil	*A Town Like Alice*	Heinemann
Smith, Dodie	*The Hundred and One Dalmatians*	Heinemann
Sperry, Armstrong	*The Boy Who Was Afraid*	Bodley Head, Knight Books, and H.E.B. (N.W.S.)
Steinbeck, John	*The Pearl*	Heinemann
Stolz, Mary	*Goodbye My Shadow*	Peacock Books
Tate, Joan	*Sam and Me*	Pan-Macmillan TOPLINERS
	The Joan Tate Books	Heinemann Educational Books
The Jet Books		Jonathan Cape
Townsend, John Rowe	*Gumble's Yard*	Hutchinson, and Puffin Books
Treece, Henry	*The Dream-Time*	Brockhampton Press
Verne, Jules	*Twenty-thousand Leagues under the Sea*	Collins, and Chatto & Windus
Wells, H. G.	*The War of the Worlds*	Penguin
Wyndham, John	*The Day of the Triffids*	Michael Joseph, and Penguin Books

Appendix B

Books for School, Public and Personal Libraries

THESE titles have been found to succeed with reluctant readers of 13+ to the extent that it is worth while including them in libraries. Again, as with the books in Appendix A, the ideal is to make them all available, and allow them to find their own level by each individual child's selection.

It has been taken for granted that copies of the traditional 'classics' will be available also, dressed in the kind of way described by Edward Blishen on page 72.

Author	*Title*	*Publisher*
Andrew, P.	*Ginger and Batty Billy* (and the Ginger books)	Lutterworth
Armstrong, R.	*Sea Change*	Dent
Avery, G.	*The Warden's Niece*	Macmillan
Bagnold, E.	*National Velvet*	Heinemann
Barrett, A.	*Songberd's Grove*	Collins
Bartos-Höppner, B.	*The Cossacks*	Oxford University Press
Bateman, R.	*Jim's First Convoy*	Brockhampton Press
Baudouy, M.	*Mick and the P.105*	Bodley Head
Baumann, H.	*I Marched with Hannibal*	Oxford University Press
Berna, Paul	*The Hundred Million Francs* *The Street Musician*	Bodley Head, and Puffin Books
Berrington, J.	*To Clear the River*	Peacock Books
Brinsmead, H. F.	*Beat of the City*	Oxford University Press
Bruckner, K.	*The Day of the Bomb*	Burke
Burnett, F. H.	*The Secret Garden*	Puffin
Cavanna, B.	*The Scarlet Sail*	Brockhampton Press
Chilton, I.	*Take Away the Flowers*	Heinemann Pyramid Books
Clarke, A. C.	*The Sands of Mars*	Sidgwick & Jackson
Clewes, D.	*A Boy like Walt*	Collins

147

Author	*Title*	*Publisher*
Cunningham, Julia	Drop Dead	Heinemann Pyramid Books
Deleeuw, A.	Give me your hand	Deutsch
Denison, M.	Susannah of the Mounties	Dent, and Puffin
Dickens, Charles	Christmas Carol	Dent and others
	Oliver Twist	Dent and others
Dillon, Eilis	The House on the Shore	Faber
	The Coriander	Faber
Douglas, O.	Penney Plain	Brockhampton Press
Duthie, E. (Ed.)	The Boy's Bedside Book of Humour	Heinemann
Forest, A.	Thursday Kidnapping	Faber
Garner, Alan	Weirdstone of Brisingamen	Collins, and
	Moon of Gomrath	Puffin Books
Garnett, E.	The Family from One End Street	Muller, and Puffin
Gayler, M.	It's a New Sound	Macdonald
George, J.	My Side of the Mountain	Bodley Head
Grahame, K.	Wind in the Willows	Methuen
Green, L.	Tales of Greek Heroes	Puffin
Guillot, R.	Kpo, the Leopard	Oxford University Press
Haggard, R.	King Solomon's Mines	Dent, and Puffin
Hamori, L.	Dangerous Journey	Constable Young Books
Heinlein, R. A.	The Red Planet	Gollancz
Hilbert, P. P.	Zoo on the First Floor	Brockhampton Press
Hildick, E. W.	Jim Starling	Chatto & Windus
	Jim Starling and the Agency	Chatto & Windus
	Jim Starling and the Colonel	Heinemann
	Jim Starling's Holiday	Heinemann
	The Jim Starling Books (for slow readers)	Blond
	The "Questers" Series	Brockhampton Press
Holm, A.	I Am David	Methuen
Household, G.	The Spanish Cave	Bodley Head, and Puffin
Hunter, N.	The Incredible Adventures of Professor Branestawm	Bodley Head, and Puffin
Inner Ring Books		Ernest Benn
James, W.	Smoky	Puffin
Johnson, A. and E.	Torrie	Brockhampton Press, and Puffin
Kastner, Erich	Emil and the Detectives	Cape, and Puffin
King, C.	Stig of the Dump	H. Hamilton, and Puffin
London, J.	White Fang	Collins
Maddock, R.	The Widgeon Gang	Collins
	The Great Bow	Collins
Marshall, J. V.	Walkabout	Peacock Books

Author	Title	Publisher
Mayne, William	*Parcel of Trees*	H. Hamilton, and Puffin
	Summer Visitors	Oxford University Press
Mitchell, Y.	*Cathy Away*	Heinemann
	Cathy at Home	Heinemann
McKown, R.	*Janine*	Macmillan
Neville, E.	*It's like this, Cat*	Harper & Row
Norton, A.	*Catseye*	Gollancz
	Night of Masks	Gollancz
Ogburn, C.	*Big Caesar*	Heinemann
Pearce, P.	*Tom's Midnight Garden*	Oxford University Press
Peyton, K. M.	*The Maplin Bird*	Oxford University Press
	The Plan for Birdsmarsh	Oxford University Press
Poe, E. A.	*Tales of Mystery and*	Dent, and
	Imagination	Penguin
Porter, G. S.	*Girl of the Limberlost*	Brockhampton Press
Ransome, A.	*Swallows and Amazons*	Cape, and
	The Coot Club	Puffin
	The Big Six	
Saville, M.	*Three Towers in Tuscany*	Heinemann
	The Purple Valley	Heinemann
	Dark Danger	Heinemann
	White Fire	Heinemann
	The Lone Pine Books	Newnes
Sellar and Yeatman	*1066 And All That*	Methuen, and Penguin
Serraillier, I.	*The Silver Sword*	Cape, and Puffin
Smith, E.	*Maiden's Trip*	MacGibbon & Kee, and
		Puffin
	Out of Hand	Macmillan
Softly, B.	*Plain Jane*	Macmillan
Steinbeck, John	*The Red Pony*	Heinemann
Stevenson, R. L.	*Treasure Island*	Puffin
Storr, C.	*Marianne and Mark*	Faber
Streatfeild, N.	*Ballet Shoes*	Dent, and Puffin
Sutcliff, R.	*The Eagle of the Ninth*	Oxford University Press
Swarthout, G. and K.	*Whichaway*	Heinemann Pyramid Books
Taylor, R.	*The Boy from Hackston N.E.*	Hamish Hamilton
Thorndike, R.	*Dr. Syn Stories*	Arrow Books
Thurber, J.	*The Thirteen Clocks and*	H. Hamilton, and Puffin
	the Wonderful O	
Townsend, J. R.	*Hell's Edge*	Hutchinson, and Puffin
	The Hallersage Sound	Hutchinson
	Widdershins Crescent	Hutchinson
Treadgold, N.	*We Couldn't Leave Dinah*	Cape
Treece, H.	*Killer in Dark Glasses*	Faber
	Bang – You're Dead!	Faber
	The Last of the Vikings	Brockhampton Press, and
		Puffin

Author	Title	Publisher
Treece, H. (*cont.*)	*The Splintered Sword*	Brockhampton Press, and Puffin
	Horned Helmet	Brockhampton Press, and Puffin
Twain, M.	*Tom Sawyer*	Puffin and others
	Huckleberry Finn	
Van Der Loeff, A. R.	*Avalanche!*	Puffin, and University of London Press
Watts, S. G.	*Number 21*	Macdonald
Windsor-Richards, A.	*There Came the Little Foxes*	Hutchinson

Appendix C
Adult Books for Young People

THESE adult novels are listed because they deal with themes and situations of interest to young people, have qualities attractive to them, and are of acceptable standard of workmanship. I would, however, wish to recall my comments on the use of adult books made at various points in this book.

Author	Title	Publisher
Asimov, I.	*Caves of Steel*	Panther Books
Baldwin, M.	*Grandad with Snails*	Secker & Warburg
Barstow, Stan	*A Kind of Loving*	Michael Joseph
Bentley, A. C.	*Trent's Last Case*	Penguin
Boulle, P.	*Bridge on the River Kwai*	Secker & Warburg
Bradbury, R.	*The Day it Rained Forever*	Hart-Davis
	The Illustrated Man	Hart-Davis
Braithwaite, E. R.	*To Sir, With Love*	Bodley Head
Brontë, E.	*Wuthering Heights*	Various
Broster, D. K.	*The Flight of the Heron*	Heinemann, and Penguin
Conrad, J.	*The Outcast of the Islands*	Dent
Crane, S.	*The Red Badge of Courage*	Hutchinson, and Heinemann New Windmill Series
Crispen, E. (Ed.)	*The Best Science Fiction 1*	Faber
Defoe, D.	*Robinson Crusoe*	Dent and others
Fleming, I.	*The James Bond Saga*	Cape, and Pan
Gallico, P.	*The Snow Goose*	Michael Joseph
	The Small Miracle	Longman's Modern Reading Series
Godden, R.	*An Episode of Sparrows*	Macmillan
Golding, W.	*Lord of the Flies*	Faber
Greene, G.	*Brighton Rock*	Heinemann, and Penguin
	Gun for Sale	Heinemann, and Penguin

Author	Title	Publisher
Hemingway, E.	*Old Man and the Sea*	Cape, and Penguin
	For Whom the Bell Tolls	Cape, and Penguin
Household, G.	*Rogue Male*	Heinemann, and Penguin
Hughes, R.	*In Hazard*	Chatto & Windus
	High Wind in Jamaica	Chatto & Windus
Knight, D.	*A Century of Science Fiction*	Gollancz
Lawrence, D. H.	*Sons and Lovers*	Heinemann
	Selected Tales	Heinemann
Leach, Christopher	*The Long Play*	W. H. Allen
Lee, Harper	*To Kill a Mockingbird*	Heinemann, and Penguin
Lee, Laurie	*Cider with Rosie*	Puffin
Llewellyn, Richard	*How Green was my Valley*	Michael Joseph
MacInnes, Colin	*Absolute Beginners*	McGibbon & Kee, and Four Square
Orwell, George	*Animal Farm*	Secker & Warburg, and
	1984	Penguin
Rawlings, M. R.	*The Yearling*	Heinemann, and Penguin
Read, Miss	*Village School*	Michael Joseph, and Penguin
Salinger, J. D.	*Catcher in the Rye*	Penguin
Sherman, D. R.	*Old Mali and the Boy*	Gollancz
Shute, Nevil	*No Highway*	Heinemann
	A Town Like Alice	Heinemann
	On the Beach	Heinemann
Sillitoe, Alan	*Saturday Night and Sunday Morning*	W. H. Allen, and Pan
Smith, Dodie	*I Captured the Castle*	Peacock Books
Steinbeck, John	*The Red Pony*	Heinemann
	The Pearl	Heinemann
	Of Mice and Men	Heinemann
Swift, Jonathan	*Gulliver's Travels*	Oxford University Press, and Constable
Waterhouse, Keith	*Billy Liar*	Michael Joseph
White, Jane	*The Wind is Green*	Deutsch
Williamson, Henry	*Tarka the Otter*	Putnam & Co. Ltd.
	Salar the Salmon	Putnam & Co. Ltd., and Puffin

Appendix D
Books for Use with Classes

A LIST of books, and series which have qualities which make them attractive to pupils in Secondary classes, and also useful for reading aloud, discussion and stimulation of the reading habit.

It is essential that the teacher using the books should have an enthusiasm for the titles used. Only if this is so will the damage we wreck in the 'study' of set texts be avoided.

There are several ways in which the books might be handled:

1. Most important, in my view, is the lesson in which a book is read aloud effectively by the teacher, as a story-telling, during which the pupils may have copies or not, as the teacher judges best. There is little discussion: it is, in fact, a performance, the teacher being the performer of the book 'script'. Such lessons should go on from the beginning of a child's life until the end of his school days, at 18 in the case of sixth formers and college people. It is a basic, staple activity.

When, as is best so, the book is short enough, the readings should be 'blanket' ones: that is, they should occupy every available lesson until the performance is over. Any discussion should wait until afterwards. Thus, as in the case of *Old Mali and The Boy*, about six to ten lessons are necessary for the performance, and only after that time has been spent, and the performance is over, should any time be spent, if the teacher judges it right, in the discussion of the interesting topics the book raises: the problem of pain, the relationship between the boy and Mali, and so on. Obviously any book of greater length than *Mali* is too long to handle like this, and should be serialised or used differently.

2. Serialisation is an obvious technique and is merely a performance given at intervals, perhaps using one lesson a week. Again the title chosen must lend itself to this device, and again, primarily, the aim should be to entertain: the corporate experience of a performance of fiction. This can be one of the

greatest stimulants to reading that reluctants are given. But it depends entirely upon the ability of the teacher to read dramatically and effectively. Not half enough time is spent in the training of teachers for this vital task.

3. A reading conducted in such a way that the story throws up ideas which are discussed at times during the reading and as they crop up in the telling. Holbrook, in *English for Maturity*, pp. 150 ff, is worth study in this context. Though Holbrook's thesis and discussion are excellent, I find his book lists somewhat 'heavy' – often difficult – for the child of average or less able intelligence.

4. The use of incidents and scenes in creative fiction to stimulate drama work after the reading; oral activity like 'programmes' of reading aloud and dramatic entertainments performed by the children themselves; painting; selection of 'incidental music' to accompany readings; and finally, of course, to stimulate fiction writing and verse making by the class. It is at this point that the selection of fiction material, and the teacher's ability to create and maintain enthusiasm, rather than merely to impose the activity, become most crucial, if the fiction itself is not to suffer the fate it has so often endured.

I must emphasise most strongly that the listed books are not intended to provide a careless and insensitive teacher with 'exercise' fodder: academic literary study of the text; grammatical and punctuation exercises; 'round-the-class' reading practice, or stop-gap material when the teacher is stuck for 'something better' to do.

Author	Title	Publisher
Bradbury, Ray	*The Veldt*, and others from *The Illustrated Man*	Hart-Davis
Chilton, Irma	*String of Time*	Pan-Macmillan TOPLINERS
Dickens, Charles	*The Christmas Carol* *Oliver Twist* (abridged)	Dent, and Heinemann
Garner, Alan	*Elidor*	Collins, and Puffin
	The Owl Service	Collins
Grahame, Kenneth	*The Wind in the Willows*	Methuen
Greene, Graham	*The Destructors* (In Twenty-one Short Stories)	Heinemann
Heinemann		Pyramid Books
Hemingway, Ernest	*The Old Man and the Sea*	Cape
	Short Stories – *The Old Man at the Bridge*	Cape
	The Nick Episodes	Cape, and Penguin

Author	Title	Publisher
Hildick, E. W.	*Louie's Lot*	Pan-Macmillan TOPLINERS
	Birdy Jones and the sequels	Pan-Macmillan TOPLINERS
Jerome, Jerome K.	Incidents from *Three Men in a Boat*	Dent
Kastner, Erich	*Emil and the Detectives*	Puffin
King, Clive	*Stig of the Dump*	Puffin
Kipling, Rudyard	*Jungle Book*	Macmillan, and Pan
	Just So Stories	Macmillan, and Pan
Lawrence, D. H.	*Stories*	Heinemann
Leach, Christopher	*Answering Miss Roberts*	Pan-Macmillan TOPLINERS
Leacock, Stephen	*Soaked in Seaweed* (From: Nonsense Novels)	Bodley Head
Lewis, C. S.	*The Lion, the Witch and the Wardrobe*	Puffin, Bles, and Collins (Evergreen)
Maddock, Reginald	*The Pit*	Collins
	Dragon in the Garden	Pan-Macmillan TOPLINERS
Marshall, J. V.	*Walkabout*	Peacock
Orwell, George	*Animal Farm*	Penguin
Poe, Edgar Allen	*Tales of Mystery and Imagination*	Dent-Everyman, and Penguin
Pope, Ray	*The Drum*	Pan-Macmillan TOPLINERS
Sherman, D. R.	*Old Mali and the Boy*	Gollancz, and Heinemann Educational Books (N.W.S.)
Sperry, Armstrong	*The Boy who was Afraid*	Bodley Head, Knight Books, and Heinemann Educational Books (N.W.S.)
Steinbeck, John	*The Pearl*	Heinemann
Tate, Joan	*Sam and Me*	Pan-Macmillan TOPLINERS
Thurber, James	*Stories from Thurber Carnival* (especially 'The Night the Bed Fell', and some of 'Fables for Our Time')	Hamish Hamilton, and Penguin
	The Thirteen Clocks and The Wonderful O	Puffin
Twain, Mark	*Huckleberry Finn*	Puffin

Author	Title	Publisher
Twain, Mark (*cont.*)	*Tom Sawyer*	Puffin
Wilde, Oscar	*The Selfish Giant* (from *The Happy Prince*)	Puffin
	The Canterville Ghost (edited)	

Appendix E
Paperback Series

A LIST of paperback series specifically directed at young people, useful both in classrooms and for private reading and possession. Only Topliners could be described as teenage books in the sense that they intend to cater for that age-group only.

Title	Publisher
Armada Books	Collins
Dragon Books	Trans Atlantic Publications
Knight Books	Brockhampton Press
Merlin Books	New English Library
Peacock and Puffin Books	Penguin Books
Topliners	Pan–Macmillan
Zebra Books	Evans Bros.

Appendix F

Review and Source Material

A LIST of available material of use in selecting books for young people.

1. Reviewing Journals

Books for your Children	4 p.a. 7s. 6d.	Ann Wood, Belvedere, 100 Church Lane East, Aldershot, Hants.
Children's Book News	6 p.a. 21s.	Children's Book Centre, 140 Kensington Church St., London W.8.
Growing Point	9 p.a. 21s.	Margery Fisher, Ashton Manor, Northampton.
Horn Book Magazine	6 p.a. 56s.	Horn Book Inc. 585 Boylston Street, Boston, Mass., U.S.A.
Junior Bookshelf	6 p.a. 21s.	Marsh Hall, Thurstonland, Huddersfield.
The School Librarian	3 p.a.	School Library Assn. Free to members of S.L.A.

The Times Educational Supplement
The Times Literary Supplement
 (Special quarterly features on children's books)
Spring and Autumn reviews in: *Spectator, Listener, New Statesman, New Society*.

2. Other Sources

Bristol University: Institute of Education	A survey of books for backward readers: 1st Survey 2nd Survey	University of London Press
Colwell, E.	*To begin with . . . A guide to reading for under 5's*	Mason
Fisher, M.	*Intent upon Reading*	Brockhampton

Lewis, N.	*The Best Children's Books of 1963*	Hamish Hamilton
Library Association	*Chosen for Children*	Library Assn.
Library Association	*Books for Young People: 11–13+, 3rd Edition*	Library Assn.
Library Association	*Books for Young People: 14–17*	Library Assn.
Library Association	*The Reluctant Reader*	Library Assn.
Lines, K.	*Four to Fourteen*	Cambridge University Press
Meek, Margaret and Culpan, Norman	*Timely Reading*	Hodder & Stoughton
National Book League	*School Library Books*	National Book League
School Library Assn.	*Primary School Library Books*	School Library Assn.
School Library Assn.	*Eleven to Fifteen*	School Library Assn.
Smith, F. S.	*An English Library: a book-man's guide.* Revised Edition	Deutsch

Appendix G
Professional Reference Books

A LIST of books professional people, particularly teachers and librarians, might find useful in relation to the topic under consideration.

Author	Title	Publisher
Alderson, Connie	*Magazines Teenagers Read*	Pergamon Press
Crouch, M. (Ed.)	*Books about Children's Literature*	Library Assn.
Crouch, M.	*Treasure Seekers and Borrowers*	Library Assn.
Education, Ministry of	*The Use of Books*	H.M.S.O.
Ellis, Alec	*How to Find out About Children's Books*	Pergamon Press
Ford, Boris (Ed.)	*Young Writers Young Readers*	Hutchinson
Green, R. L.	*Tellers of Tales* Revised Edition	Ward
Grimshaw, E.	*The Teacher Librarian*	E. J. Arnold
Hoggart, Richard	*The Uses of Literacy*	Chatto & Windus, and Penguin
Holbrook, D.	*English for Maturity*	Cambridge University Press
Kamm, Antony and Taylor, Boswell	*Books and the Teacher*	University of London Press
Linden, R. O.	*Books and Libraries*	Cassell
McColvin, L. R.	*Libraries for Children*	Phoenix
Purton, R.	*Surrounded by Books*	E.S.A.
Ralph, R. G.	*The Library in Education*	Phoenix
Roe, E.	*Teachers, Librarians and Children: A study of Libraries in Education*	Crosby Lockwood
Sampson, G.	*English for the English*	Cambridge University Press
School Library Assn.	*The Library in the Primary School*	S.L.A.
School Library Assn.	*Using Books in the Primary School*	S.L.A.
Smith, A. E.	*English in the Modern School*	Methuen

Author	Title	Publisher
Stott, C. A.	*School Libraries: A Short Manual*	Cambridge University Press
Townsend, John Rowe	*Written for Children*	Garnet Miller
Trease, G.	*Tales out of School*	Heinemann Educational Books